CW00546820

THE TRENT VALLEY RAILWAY

MIKE HITCHES

Sutton Publishing Limited
Phoenix Mill · Thrupp · Stroud
Gloucestershire · GL5 2BU

First published 2003

Title page photograph: Ex-Midland Railway 3F 0–6–0 at the head of a local train at Abbey Street station on 14 April 1957. *(H.C. Casserley)*

British Library Cataloguing in Publication Data
A catalogue record for this book is available from the British Library.

ISBN 0-7509-3046-2

Typeset in 10.5/13.5 Photina.
Typesetting and origination by Sutton Publishing Limited.
Printed and bound in England by J.H. Haynes & Co. Ltd, Sparkford.

To Paul and Roma

ACKNOWLEDGEMENTS

I should like to record my grateful thanks to all who have patiently assisted me in my efforts to prepare this book. I have received much help from staffs at Staffordshire Record Office, Stafford; Warwickshire Record Office, Warwick; Wolverhampton Record Office; Nuneaton Library and Lichfield Library. They have all shown great kindness when dealing with my many enquiries and it has been very much appreciated.

Individual assistance has been given by the late Arthur Truby, Tim Shuttleworth, Roger Carpenter, Jim Roberts, David Ibbotson and the Revd David Hardy. Without their help this project would have been far more difficult to complete. My thanks also go to Glad Stockdale for redrawing my plans.

Finally, I should like to thank my late wife Alwen, who was very involved in this project when it was first under way. Also many thanks to Hilary who has been very supportive and to my son Gary who has shown much interest.

CONTENTS

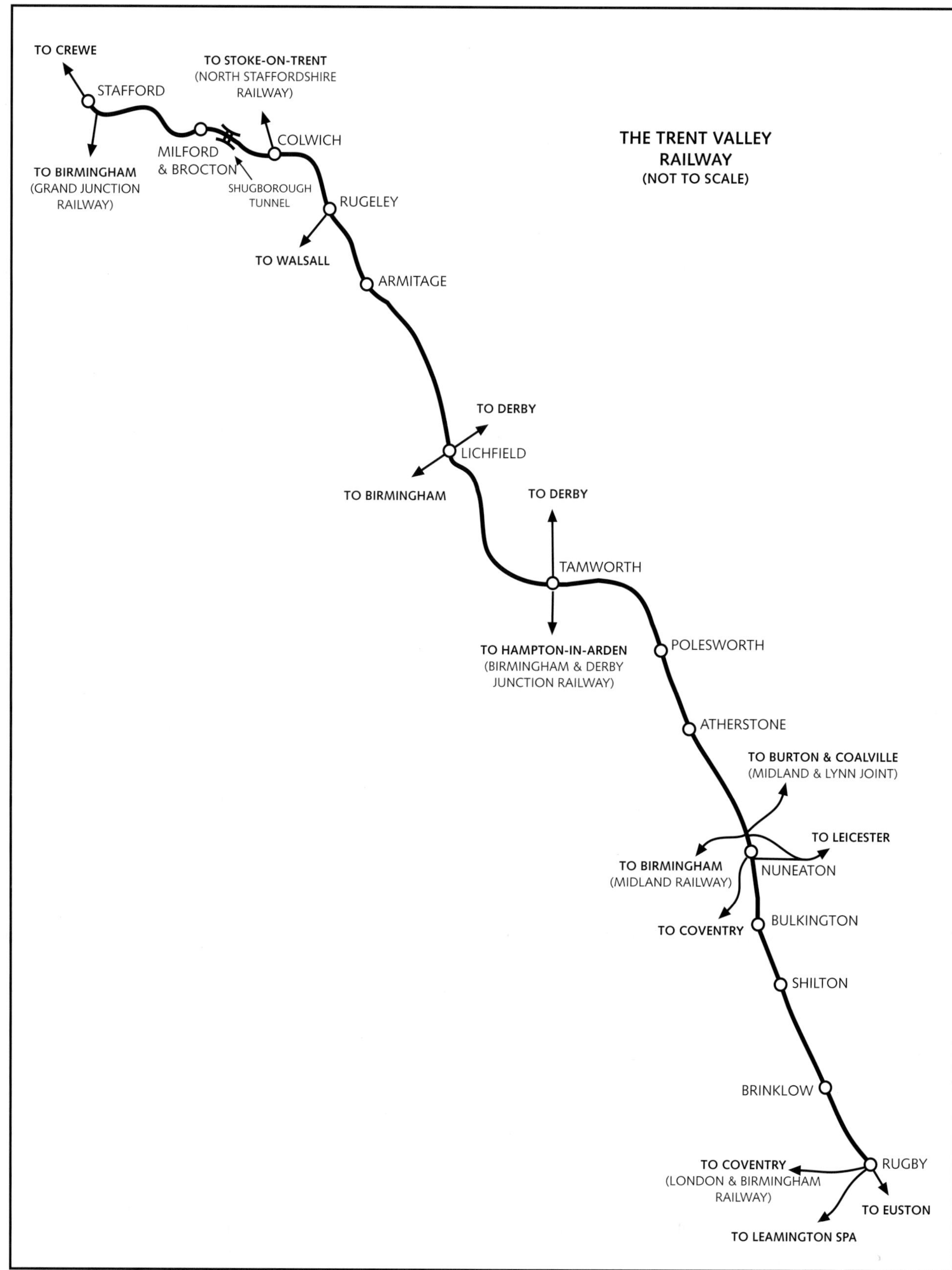
THE TRENT VALLEY
RAILWAY
(NOT TO SCALE)
TO CREWE
STAFFORD
TO BIRMINGHAM
(GRAND JUNCTION
RAILWAY)
MILFORD
& BROCTON
SHUGBOROUGH
TUNNEL
TO STOKE-ON-TRENT
(NORTH STAFFORDSHIRE
RAILWAY)
COLWICH
RUGELEY
TO WALSALL
ARMITAGE
TO DERBY
LICHFIELD
TO BIRMINGHAM
TO DERBY
TAMWORTH
TO HAMPTON-IN-ARDEN
(BIRMINGHAM & DERBY
JUNCTION RAILWAY)
POLESWORTH
ATHERSTONE
TO BURTON & COALVILLE
(MIDLAND & LYNN JOINT)
TO LEICESTER
TO BIRMINGHAM
(MIDLAND RAILWAY)
NUNEATON
TO COVENTRY
BULKINGTON
SHILTON
BRINKLOW
TO COVENTRY
(LONDON & BIRMINGHAM
RAILWAY)
RUGBY
TO EUSTON
TO LEAMINGTON SPA

INTRODUCTION

Running between Stafford and Rugby, the Trent Valley Railway was to become the most strategically important route in the West Midlands, providing a bypass line which avoided the congested railway network in the rapidly expanding industrial town of Birmingham. So fast was the growth of Birmingham that it was given city status in 1889, and went on to become the second largest city in England. Birmingham businessmen, however, were not interested in investing in the new railways, as they sold their products at the factory gate, and it was up to the purchaser to arrange his own transport. Investment, generally, came from men of importance in Liverpool, which goes some way to explain why the great Midlands industrial conurbation was only an interchange point on the railway network, a role it still assumes today.

Following the success of the first true 'InterCity' passenger-carrying railway, the Liverpool & Manchester Railway, which had opened, fully steam-hauled, on 15 September 1830 and showed a profit of £14,432 in its first three-and-a-half months of existence, two companies proposed building trunk routes, linking London with the major seaports of the north-west, their respective lines connecting at Curzon Street station, Birmingham. The main station building at Curzon Street still exists, albeit now in the middle of a goods yard, and can be seen from London-bound trains leaving New Street station, which had been built by the London & North Western Railway to replace it. The two companies, the London & Birmingham Railway and Grand Junction Railway, received royal assent to construct their respective routes on 6 May 1833. The L&B was originally intended to operate between Camden and Birmingham, but was extended down a steep bank to Euston by Act of Parliament on 3 July 1835. The GJR line ran between Birmingham and Earlstown, Lancashire, where it connected with the Liverpool & Manchester Railway for access to the great seaport of Liverpool.

The GJR line was the first to open, on 4 July 1837, being much more easily built than the L&B route, which involved the major construction of Kilsby Tunnel, and had important stations at Warrington and Stafford, as well as a small station in an out-of-the-way location at Wolverhampton. The L&B was opened, with a limited service advertised, all the way between Euston and Curzon Street from 24 June 1838, its important stations being at Bletchley, Rugby and Coventry. Full service on the L&B commenced on 17 September 1838.

With the opening of the GJR and L&B railway trunk routes linking London with Liverpool, Birmingham became the hub with all interchange facilities being provided at Curzon Street. The companies closely cooperated in their efforts to gain traffic between the north-west and the capital. So successful were these ventures that railway traffic poured into the West Midlands, causing a great deal of congestion. The busy nature of the area was emphasised in a report by a body set up to investigate proposals drawn up during the 'Railway Mania' period, when the war between the 7ft gauge of the GWR and the 4ft 8½in of the other companies was at its height. In 1845 this committee felt that if there were any unavoidable breaks between the competing gauges, then these should be at Bristol or Oxford, where traffic was lightest, rather than at busy traffic centres such as Rugby, Wolverhampton, Birmingham and Gloucester.

The two main trunk routes actually formed two sides of a triangle, the L&B running east–west, while the GJR ran approximately south–north, and it became apparent that the third side of the triangle, through the Trent Valley, would very soon be necessary to carry through traffic between London and the north-west of England, and away from congested Birmingham. The need for a bypass line became even more urgent as the railway network in the north-west expanded further, with the opening of the Chester & Crewe Railway, and the Chester & Birkenhead Railway in 1840. The

Manchester & Birmingham Railway followed in 1842, and proposals were made for a railway between Chester and the Irish Sea port at Holyhead in 1844, the line actually opening in 1848.

At this time the Secretary of the GJR was one Captain Mark Huish. He was destined to play perhaps the most important role in the development of the Trent Valley Railway, and of all the railways within his orbit, over the next few years. His manner of dealing with other parties became apparent during a dispute with Pickford's over carriage rates, which dragged on for months, and this steeled the man to tackle anyone who dared to challenge his railway interests. Thus, as plans were being formulated for a new bypass line, he set about ensuring that his own interests would not suffer, and was prepared to go to any lengths to have his own way. This led to one of the great railway disputes of the early railway age, and one that the good Captain was determined to win.

An early attempt was made by the embryonic Birmingham & Manchester Railway to build a line through the Trent Valley. Its projected 8-mile route, from Stone in Staffordshire to Rugby, was promoted in 1839 as a line to London that would be independent of Captain Huish's GJR. It was to have a branch from Lichfield to the Midland Railway at Alrewas, and was of great interest to businessmen in the Potteries. The scheme, however, failed to gain parliamentary approval, but the concept of a direct route between the north-west, the Potteries and London, bypassing Birmingham, was kept alive by interested parties in the Potteries. They found plenty of local support for a line through the Trent Valley, including a number of influential people who met at Nuneaton. They agreed that a line through the Trent Valley 'will be of the greatest advantage to the Town and Neighbourhood, in affording the Inhabitants there of the readiest communication with the Metropolis, and also, with the great commercial Towns of Manchester and Liverpool and other places on the line, and by that means facilitating the sale of extensive manufactured Silk, Cotton, and Worsted Goods, as well as the numerous mineral productions of this and the adjoining parishes.' The promoters were thinking in particular of Hinckley, Bedworth and Bulkington, which were centres of these manufacturing trades.

To further the aspirations of the promoters, an independent company was formed in 1843 with Edward Watkin appointed as Secretary. Two years after the formation of the Trent Valley Railway Company, arrangements were made for the L&B to lease the line, which was to run between Stafford and Rugby, although the original intention was for the lease to reach only as far as Tamworth, from Rugby. The agreement was, however, made in haste so that a Bill for construction could be entered into parliament as soon as possible.

The promoters of the Trent Valley Railway revived their scheme in 1845, and proposed two branches from the TVR, between Armitage and Wichnor, and from Stafford to Stoke. (The latter was also being pressed by the GJR.) Both branches were soon dropped from the proposal. The L&B, however, was preparing to expand its interests by provisionally agreeing to absorb the Manchester & Birmingham Railway, and the Trent Valley Railway, as well as the Churnet Valley line in North Staffordshire, if it was established.

The various Trent Valley Railway proposals caused a major rift in previously friendly relations between the GJR and L&B, the latter regarding such a line as a convenient bypass away from Birmingham, where rail congestion was becoming a serious problem, and as a useful route to Manchester. The GJR immediately went on the defensive, because this new, independent route would deprive it of Manchester traffic, and it would also lose Potteries traffic once the new line was established. Secretary of the GJR Captain Mark Huish was not going to allow his company to be deprived of traffic in this way, and began to plot against the L&B, as well as the M&B and TVR, in his efforts to retain traffic levels for his company.

Huish wanted to force the L&B to the negotiating table, and one sure way to alarm the Euston company was to make approaches to the broad gauge Great Western Railway, whose 7ft gauge would cause a break of gauge with the L&B at Rugby. To achieve the desired result, Huish tried to persuade the GWR to build a line of their own from the Birmingham terminus at Curzon Street to join the

GWR Oxford branch, which had been opened in 1840. The tracks were to join at Rugby. Just to ruffle the L&B's feathers even more, Huish argued that bringing the broad gauge into Rugby would 'avoid all curses of monopoly'.

The project was supported by the ironmasters, merchants and manufacturers of Birmingham, who were less than happy with the L&B's alleged abuse of its monopoly, especially in its handling of goods traffic – charging extortionate rates and refusing to supply much-needed additional accommodation. The directors of the GWR resisted Huish's approaches for some time, the L&B's hostility towards their plans to build a railway from Oxford to Rugby, and the efforts being made by the Midland Railway to displace the broad gauge from Gloucester to Bristol by purchasing the Birmingham & Bristol Railway and by making passenger and freight transfer between the two track gauges as difficult as possible, led the GWR to believe that no friendly interchange of traffic would be possible. As a result the GWR gave wholehearted support to the new project, which was to be broad gauge. The GJR even went as far as proposing to add broad gauge rails on their own lines to Liverpool and Manchester, and had estimates of cost made by their engineer. Unfortunately the GWR were not aware of Huish's plot to force the L&B into negotiations, and were destined to be the eventual losers in the GJR Secretary's power game.

By a Subscribers' Agreement of 15 April 1845 power was given to enter into contracts for sale or lease of the Oxford–Rugby line to the GJR and GWR, each being empowered to nominate three members to a committee. Stipulations were made for securing the railway as a rival to the L&B and keeping it out of the L&B's hands. Later, when sanction of the Oxford and Rugby line by parliament was assured, a line, projected to run from Oxford to Birmingham, was shortened to join the new line at Knightcote, 2 miles north of Fenny Compton, instead of connecting with the GWR at Oxford.

Not only did the GJR actively promote a rival route to that of the L&B, but it obtained authority to subscribe a large amount of capital to the Trent Valley Railway project, in exchange for full running powers, under the Trent Valley Authorisation Act of 1845. With the GJR in such a strong position, the L&B had little choice but to come to terms with Huish, who in turn deserted the GWR, having no further need to compete with the Euston company. In addition, Huish, who had spoken of trying to avoid monopoly situations when in dispute with the L&B, was very keen to maintain a monopoly now that it suited him, and the GWR was soon to find itself up against a sworn enemy, particularly when the Paddington company tried to construct its line from London to Birmingham – something Huish had supported when in dispute with the L&B – and he did all he could to prevent the GWR competing for traffic in the West Midlands town. The line between Oxford and Rugby, which had been used as the lever to force the L&B into line, was never to materialise.

Once matters had been resolved between the GJR and the various companies involved in promoting the Trent Valley Railway, shareholders of the M&B revolted against their board and formed a committee to negotiate better terms with the L&B. Many held interests in both companies and were heartily sick of the disputes between the railways, feeling that friendly relations would be more beneficial to all. This was to be the prelude to the formation of the mighty London & North Western Railway, the new company coming into existence on 16 July 1846. The general manager of the new company was none other than the redoubtable Captain Mark Huish.

Buoyed by his victory over the L&B and the TVR, Huish went on to flex his muscles against other companies that had the temerity to challenge the new LNWR's monopoly in its natural territory in the north-west of England. His battles were epitomised by his struggles with two small but resilient companies based in Shrewsbury, the Shrewsbury & Birmingham Railway and the Shrewsbury & Chester Railway, which had come to an agreement for handling through traffic from Birmingham to the north-west of England in direct competition with the LNWR. The two companies stoutly resisted all Huish's conniving and often illegal attempts to force them into submission. They eventually joined forces with the captain's sworn enemy, the GWR, giving the Paddington company access to lucrative traffic from Merseyside docks, something Huish had sought to avoid. By 1854 Huish had been beaten, and he faded into history. He left a legacy of bad feeling between Euston and Paddington which was to last for quite a few years. On the other hand he did bring about the establishment of what was to become the largest joint stock company in the world, the LNWR, with assets greater than some nations, and he had a hand in the development of the Trent Valley Railway which considerably shortened journey times between Euston and the north-west of England.

THE TRENT VALLEY RAILWAY

Royal assent for construction of the Trent Valley Railway was given on 21 July 1845, and it provided for a capital of £1,250,000 in £20 shares; there was also provision to raise loan capital of £416,000. The first sod was cut at Camel Close, half a mile or so from Tamworth, in the following November by Prime Minister Sir Robert Peel, who was MP for Tamworth from 1830 until his death twenty years later. In his speech he thanked local landowners for their cooperation: 'I assure them that there are many persons in this neighbourhood who have not scrupled to sacrifice private feeling and comfort, by consenting to their land being appropriated to the Trent Valley Railway. They have given that consent from a conviction that the undertaking was one conducive to the public benefit, and that consideration of private interest should not obstruct the great one of the public good.' Despite Peel's fine words, there can be little doubt that these landowners extracted a more than fair price from the railway company for use of their land, as was common practice in those early railway days. When the L&B sought royal assent for its line, landowners opposed to the Bill were only appeased by the payment of three times the true land values. Indeed, some made fortunes from the sale of only small parcels of land for railway development. No doubt high land prices made it difficult for railway companies to invest in improvements to the infrastructure, or to spend extensively on locomotives and rolling stock, as so much of their capital had been spent in acquiring the land on which to build the railway in the first place.

In April 1846 the Trent Valley Railway Company was bought outright by the L&B, GJR and M&B, and construction was well under way when the LNWR was formed. The railway's engineers were Robert Stephenson and George Bidder, with T.L. Gooch in charge. The contractor for the line was the famous Thomas Brassey, who had already been involved in several major railway contracts, one being worth some £4.3 million for the construction of 118 miles of line, and he had a total labour force of some 45,000 men. The major engineering feature of the new line was the 774-yard Shugborough Tunnel between Colwich and Stafford. Its flamboyant portals earned it the nickname 'The Gates of Jerusalem'. Due to the narrowness of the valley floor, the River Trent had to be spanned several times, and bridges were a feature of the line.

On completion, the new line was scheduled for opening on 26 June 1847, and there were celebrations, in spectacular style, with guests banqueting at Tamworth. Some of these guests, including Robert Stephenson, had been brought by special train from Euston to Rugby, where a Midland Railway train, carrying the future 'Railway King' George Hudson and George Stephenson, was waiting, along with another special train from Birmingham. The whole party then proceeded along the new line to Tamworth, where trains from Liverpool and Manchester were waiting. All the guests were welcomed by Sir Robert Peel, and a substantial dinner was provided in a large marquee near the station. Around 1,300 people listened to the various speeches. The future 'Railway King' was reputed to have behaved rather badly during the event.

The opening celebrations, however, proved somewhat premature. Concern was expressed about six of the railway bridges. Constructed using cast-iron, they were similar to the one built for the Chester & Holyhead Railway that spanned the River Dee at Chester. Opened in about 1846, this bridge collapsed in quite spectacular fashion in May 1847 under a Shrewsbury to Chester train, killing six passengers. The CHR was not to open until 1848, but the section between Saltney Junction and Chester was already being used by the Shrewsbury & Chester Railway, which had running powers for access to the Roman city. A cast-iron replacement for the collapsed bridge, designed by Robert Stephenson, was opened later in the same year, but it was found to be of poor design and the whole structure was extensively rebuilt, using wrought iron and brick, in 1871. Little wonder, then, that there was a reluctance to open the Trent Valley line while cast-iron bridges were under such suspicion.

The new line had been inspected by Captain Joshua Coddington (later the Secretary of the Caledonian Railway) in the declining months of 1847, and his report was favourable to the opening of the Trent Valley Railway. The government, however, had appointed a commission to study cast-iron bridges, and although Coddington was happy to allow the line to open, the Railway Commissioners requested a further inspection. Coddington stuck to his belief that the line was ready to take traffic, and the first goods trains, along with two local passenger trains, began operations on 15 September 1847. The route, however, was not fully used until the beginning of December. The iron bridges were replaced when the line was widened.

The final delay was not of the LNWR's making, but was due to the Post Office, which was in dispute with Euston over both the timing and the diversion of mail trains. Before the opening of the Trent Valley Railway, mail trains between London and the north-west ran along the L&B to Birmingham, where mails were transferred, and then along the GJR for the journey north, the train leaving Euston at 8.30pm. When the mail trains began operating along the TVR, mail transfer took place at Tamworth, the point where the Midland Railway's line between Sheffield, Derby, Birmingham and Bristol crossed the LNWR route between London and the north-west. Mail trains using the Trent Valley route left Euston at 8.45pm instead of 8.30, the train then being known as the 'North Western TPO', and ran as far as Preston. The Up train to Euston left Preston at 8.23pm, arriving in London at 4.50am. The Down train was timed to arrive in Tamworth at 12.25am, while the Up train arrived at 12.42am. Over the years this train was extended to Glasgow and Aberdeen, responsibility for operation being shared between the LNWR and Caledonian Railway. From 22 August 1923, following the 'Grouping' of that year, the train became the Down and Up Special TPO and carried no passengers. It still operated via the Trent Valley line, leaving Euston at 8.30pm. The Down Special was made famous in the documentary film *Night Mail*, which was made for the Post Office and LMS railway in 1935. The Special TPOs continued to use the Trent Valley route until the 1960s when, because of electrification work, the Sunday Down mail ran via Birmingham, departing Euston at 8pm. From 6 March 1967, when electrification of the Birmingham lines was completed, both Down and Up Mail Specials were permanently re-routed via Birmingham, thereby reverting to their original route and away from the Trent Valley. Mail from the West Country joined the Special in Birmingham instead of Tamworth.

Commenting on the delays to the full opening of the Trent Valley Railway, G.C. Glyn, chairman of the LNWR, told the half-yearly meeting in February 1846: 'Owing to imperfect consolidation of the new Line of Way, and to the unfavourable weather, for some time after the opening the journeys were performed with less regularity than along the old route by Birmingham.'

With full opening on 1 December 1847, Standard Time arrangements had been introduced to coincide with operation of mail trains over the TVR. Until then Birmingham, for example, had local time some seven minutes behind Greenwich. Glyn stated in the half-yearly meeting: 'The opening, and the new Post Office arrangements required for the conveyance of Mails by that line, afforded a favourable opportunity for introducing uniformity between Railway and Post Office time; and for regulating the expression of all local time, as far as practicable, in conformity with the longitude of Greenwich.'

At its opening, the Trent Valley Railway was provided with eleven intermediate stations, each having its own individual character and all designed by architect John Livock, who had also designed stations on the L&B line to Peterborough. The stations were at Colwich, Rugeley, Armitage, Lichfield, Tamworth, Polesworth, Atherstone, Nuneaton, Bulkington, Shilton and Stretton. So called 'First Class' stations were at Atherstone, Tamworth (the important mail exchange point and parliamentary seat of Sir Robert Peel) and Lichfield. Rather surprisingly, given its future role as an important junction,

Nuneaton was not given First Class status at opening. At Second Class stopping places less money had been spent on passenger accommodation and the quality of the station buildings. The First Class stations were conveniently sited to serve as many 'country seats' as possible. Atherstone station, for example, was within easy reach of Merevale, Atherstone, Sheepy and Gapsall Halls and Cliffe House. In its heyday, the station would have witnessed a great deal of coming and going of the nobility, with their servants and carriages. The First Class stations were substantially built of stone with brick façades, and tall chimneys, of ornate style, were very much the norm. Interiors were roomy, with all the facilities that passengers would require, and the approach roads were wide. All the stations were in a Jacobean style of architecture and built with stone.

Once the Trent Valley line had opened, journey times between Liverpool and London were reduced to six hours, but the new line relegated Birmingham and the Black Country to second place in the LNWR timetable, because most passengers to and from Birmingham were forced to change at Rugby. Travellers complained bitterly about these inconveniences until 1870 when, to suit its own purposes, rather than addressing the public need, the LNWR split the overloaded expresses between Euston and the north-west. Liverpool and Manchester were each given their own train, these carrying portions for Coventry and Birmingham, as well as Wolverhampton. Birmingham was also given three daily expresses from Euston, the fastest being five minutes short of three hours.

The new Trent Valley route proved a great success, avoiding as it did the congested West Midlands and significantly reducing journey times between London and the north-west's major towns. It continued to be the most important line on the LNWR and prospered for many years, with the most famous express trains operating over the route.

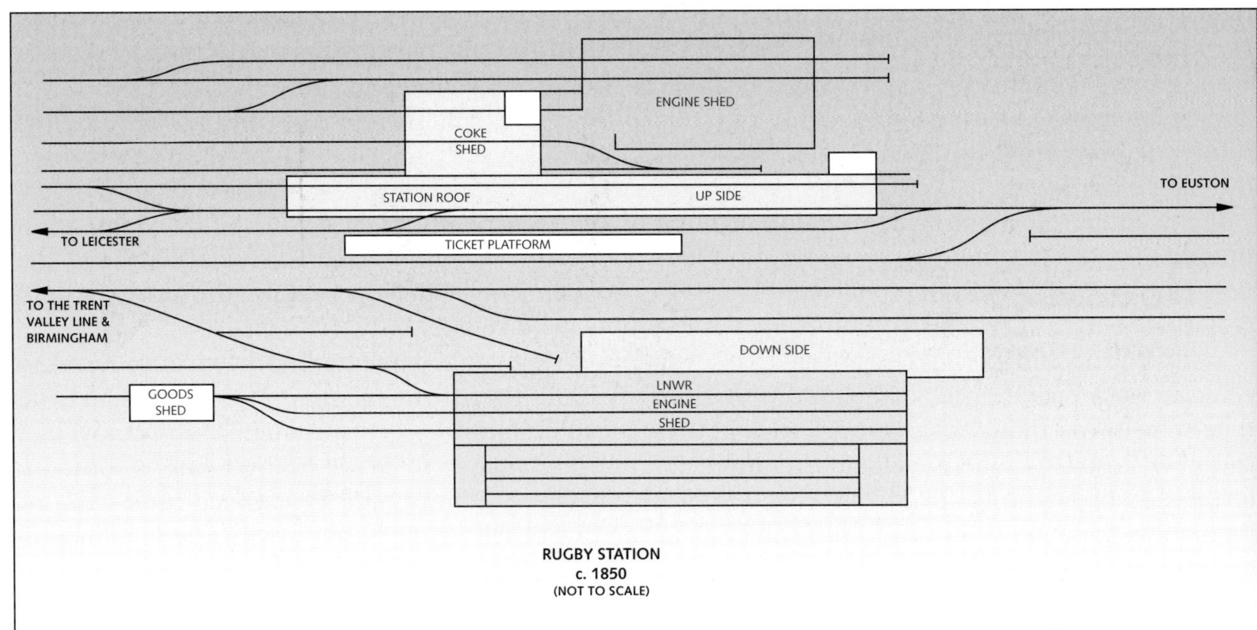

A plan of Rugby station as it appeared in 1850. This was the original station when the Trent Valley Railway opened. A small engine shed was opened here by the LNWR, but was not large enough to cope with the demands placed upon it with the opening of the TVR and another was opened opposite, as can be seen here. The new station was itself to become inadequate for the demands placed upon it and it was superseded by another in the 1880s. *(Author)*

1

The Trent Valley Railway

Rugby has been provided with a station since the opening of the London & Birmingham Railway in 1838. The original station, at Old Station Square, was replaced in 1840 when the Midland Counties Railway, from Nottingham, Derby and Leicester, completed its eleven-arch viaduct to join the L&B. This station was itself replaced in 1851, following the opening of a line from Market Harborough and a local line from Leamington Spa. It was only to last until 1886 when the LNWR opened a completely new Rugby station some 90 yards closer to London than its predecessor. The not insubstantial sum of £70,000 was allotted by the LNWR to build it. The station, seen here in about 1910, was basically a very large island, 470 yards long and 37 yards wide, with bays at each end, and covered by a pitched roof which continued longitudinally over the bay platforms. As protection against the elements, a vertical glass screen was placed between the roof support columns. Station notices were at right angles to the platform face. This rebuilt station still serves Rugby today. *(F.W. Shuttleworth Collection)*

Waiting at Rugby station in about 1900 is a Manchester-bound express, headed by an unidentified Francis Webb-designed 'Benbow' Class 4–4–0. This train would have started its journey from Euston and would head up the TVR to Colwich where it would join the North Staffordshire Railway route, via Stoke-on-Trent, to Manchester (London Road), now Manchester Piccadilly. *(Author's Collection)*

A general view of Rugby station, *c.* 1900. The platform is crowded with parcel carts, station staff and passengers. At the platform is a Birmingham-bound train headed by one of Webb's famous 'Precedent' Class 2–4–0 locomotives, better known as 'Jumbos'. When the TVR first opened, passengers for Coventry, Birmingham and Wolverhampton had to change at Rugby, which caused some upset. The LNWR eventually took notice and northbound trains were equipped with special coaches that were detached at Rugby for onward journey to the West Midlands. *(Author's Collection)*

The famous Rugby signal gantry, shown here under construction, stood just in front of the viaduct, itself still being built, which carried the Great Central Railway route from Marylebone through Rugby Central to the north-east of England. In the background is Rugby no. 1 signal-box. This gantry stood at Rugby from 1898 until 1939. The upper signal layer was simply a duplicate of the lower. From left to right the signals controlled the Down fast to goods, through fast, fast to platform, slow to goods, slow to fast, slow to platform, slow to Bay One, slow to Bay Two, Market Harborough goods, Market Harborough fast, Market Harborough platform, Market Harborough Bay One and Market Harborough Bay Two. The Down goods line passed to the left and was not signalled from this gantry. *(F.W. Shuttleworth Collection)*

Rugby station staff in the 1890s, showing off their LNWR uniforms. In the middle at the front are the stationmaster and his assistant suitably attired in top hats. *(F.W. Shuttleworth Collection)*

Rugby station's north platform, *c.* 1917. Passengers are disembarking from a local train in the distance. *(Author's Collection)*

Table 30 SUMMARY TABLES

Table 30

LONDON and SCOTLAND

WEEKDAYS

	CR am	R am	R am	am S	XR am	PR am	R am S	HR am	BR am	R am	R am	R am	Q am M	W am	FR pm	Q pm Y
LONDON (Euston) .... dep									10 0		10 7	10 20			1 0	
,, (King's Cross) ,,	1 0	4 0			9 30		9 50	10 0		10 5			11 30	11 45		1 10
,, (St. Pancras).. ,,			8 50	9 0		9 40										
	am	pm	pm	pm	pm	pm	pm	pm	pm	pm	pm	pm	pm	pm	pm	pm
Edinburgh (Princes St.) .. arr											6E55	7 40			9 45	
,, (Waverley) .. ,,	9 35	1 45	7 24		5 10		6 12	5e54		6 27			7 35	8 9		9 23
Glasgow (Central) ...... ,,									6 25		7 0				9 45	
,, (Queen St.) .. ,,	11 9	3 8	10d9		7 15		7 58	7 58		7 58			8 56	9 20		11 34
,, (St. Enoch) .... ,,				7 40		7 55									am	
Perth (General) .. .. ,,	11 48	3 37			8 28		8 28	8 28		8 28		8 52	12a12	12ay7	12A21	12a12
Dundee (Tay Bridge)...... ,,	11 40	3 55	10t58		7 7		8 25	8 25		8 25			11 6	10t58		12a48
,, (West) .. .. ,,												10 28				
Aberdeen .... ,,	1p35	5 53			9 25		10 23	10 23		10 23		11S22			3A19	
Inverness .. .. .. ,,	3p38	8 2													5A20	

WEEKDAYS—*continued*

	R pm	pm AA	R pm FX	R pm FO	LR pm FX	LR pm FO	DR pm E	DR pm E	DR pm S	pm K	pm	D pm E	D pm S	J pm E	J pm S	D pm
LONDON (Euston) .. dep							7 20	7 30	7 30			9 5	9 5			
,, (King's Cross) ,,	2 0	6 45	6 55	6 55	7 5	7 5					8 20					
,, (St. Pancras).. ,,										7 55				9 0	9 0	9 10
	pm	am	am	am	am	am	am	am	am	am	am	am	am	am	am	am
Edinburgh (Princes St.) .. arr																
,, (Waverley) .. ,,	10 7	3 23	3 23	3 40	3 40	4 0					6 8			7 42	7 42	
Glasgow (Central) .. ,,												5 55	6 0			
,, (Queen Street) .. ,,	11 34				5f20	5 20					7g38			9 20	12p27	
,, (St. Enoch) .. ,,										6 56						8 30
Perth (General) .... ,,	12ay7				8f45	8 45	4 55	6 10	6 30		8g45			10 39		
Dundee (Tay Bridge) .. ,,	12SUa48	5 2	5 2	5 22	5 22	5 42					8g57			11 12	1p40	
,, (West) .... ,,								7 3	10 8							
Aberdeen .. .. .. ,,		6 57	6k57	7 19	7 19	7 38	7 46	8 15	11 39		11g16			1 35		
Inverness .... ,,	5A 20						9 34	10 6	12b44		2SUp5			3p38		

WEEKDAYS—*continued*

	D pm	GR pm E	NR pm S	V pm T	pm U	C pm E	C pm S	DR pm E	DR pm S	DR pm E
LONDON (Euston) .. dep	9 25							10 50	11 25	11 40
,, (King's Cross) ,,		10§15	10 15	10 20	10 20	10 30	10 30			
,, (St. Pancras).. ,,										
	am	am	am	am	am	am	am	am	am	am
Edinburgh (Princes St.) .. arr	7Z58							8 54	8 55	
,, (Waverley) .. ,,		6 21	6 21	6 36	6 36	7 4	7 16			
Glasgow (Central) .. ,,	7 36								9 5	9 30
,, (Queen Street) .. ,,		8 47	9 3	8 47	9 3	8 47	9 3			
,, (St. Enoch) .. ,,										
Perth (General) .... ,,		9 14	9 23	9 14	9 23	9 14	9 23	9 27		
Dundee (Tay Bridge) .. ,,		8 57	9 19	8 57	9 19	9 18	9 19			
,, (West) .... ,,								11 4		
Aberdeen .. .. .. ,,		11 16	11 22	11 16	11 22	11 16	11 22	1p52		
Inverness .... ,,		3p38	2p 5		2p 5		2p 5	3p38		

A—Except Sunday mornings.
AA—Fridays only, 14th July to 1st September inclusive.
a—Morning time.
B—THE ROYAL SCOT.
b—On 11th June arrives Inverness 2.5 pm.
C—Limited Sleeping accommodation.
D—1st and 3rd class Sleeping accommodation.
d—Passengers can arrive Glasgow 9.20 pm by Pullman Car Train from Edinburgh. Supplementary charges.
E—Except Saturdays.
e—On Saturdays arrives Edinburgh (Waverley) 5.58 pm.
F—THE MID-DAY SCOT. FO—Fridays only.
FX—Fridays excepted. f—Except Sundays.
G—THE NIGHT SCOTSMAN. Limited Sleeping accommodation to Edinburgh and Dundee.
g—On Sunday mornings arrive Glasgow 9.3 am, Perth 9.23 am, Dundee 9.19 am, Aberdeen 11.22 am.
H—THE FLYING SCOTSMAN.
J—1st and 3rd class Sleeping accommodation. Does not convey Sleeping Car passengers from London to Edinburgh.
K—Fridays only. Commences 30th June.
k—On Sundays arrives 7.3 am.
L—THE ABERDONIAN. Limited Sleeping accommodation.
M—Saturdays only, 17th June to 9th September inclusive.
N—THE NIGHT SCOTSMAN. Limited Sleeping accommodation to Edinburgh.
P—THE THAMES-CLYDE EXPRESS.
p—Afternoon time. Q—Buffet Car.
R—Restaurant Car whole or part of journey.
S—Saturdays only.
SU—Sundays only.
T—Mondays and Fridays only.
t—On Saturdays arrives 11.6 pm.
U—Saturdays only. Commences 1st July.
V—Third Class sleeping accommodation.
W—THE QUEEN OF SCOTS. Pullman Cars only, King's Cross to Glasgow. Supplementary charges.
X—THE CAPITALS LIMITED. NON-STOP King's Cross to Edinburgh (Wav.).
Y—Saturdays only, 24th June to 9th September inclusive.
y—Arrives 5 minutes later on Saturdays.
Z—On Sunday mornings arrives Edinburgh (Princes Street) 7.50 am.
§—Conveys only Sleeping Car passengers for Edinburgh and Dundee and ordinary passengers for stations beyond Edinburgh.

Heavy figures indicate Through Carriages from London.

SUMMARY TABLES Table 30

Table 30—*continued*

SCOTLAND and LONDON

WEEKDAYS

	XR am	HR pm	BR am	R am	R am	am S	R am Y	R pm	PR am	U am	R pm	am b	R am	FR am M	FR pm N	R am Q
Inverness .... dep		11h20						11h20			11h20			8 20		8 20
Aberdeen .. .. .. ,,	5 55	5a55			5 55		5 55	6a25			5a55	8 0	9 55	9 35		9 35
Dundee (Tay Bridge) .... ,,	7 45	7a45			7 45		7 45			8 35	7 45	9 53	11 50			
,, (West) .. .. ,,								7 52						11 35		11 35
Perth (General) .... ,,	6 15	6a15			8 15		8 15	8 55		9 7	8 15	9 7	12p10	12p14		12p14
Glasgow (Central) .. ,,			10 0	10 6										1p15	1 15	
,, (Queen Street) .. ,,	7 30	7a30			8 35		9 8			10 30	8 35	11 50	12r 0			
,, (St. Enoch) .. ,,						9 0			9 20							
Edinburgh (Princes Street) ,,				10 12										1p 0		1p 0
,, (Waverley) .. ,,	9 45	10a 0			10 15		10 32			11 40	10 10	1p25	2p 0			
	pm	pm	pm	pm	pm	pm	pm	pm	pm	pm	pm	pm	pm	pm	pm	pm
LONDON (Euston) .. arr			6 13	6 54				7 12						10 9	10 9	11Q11
,, (King's Cross) ,,	5 30	6 0			6 47		7 3			8 10		10 0	10 10			
,, (St. Pancras) .. ,,						7 17			7 28		9 17					

WEEKDAYS—*continued*

	R am	R pm	R am	R pm	R pm A	m pm K	pm FO	C pm	D pm	GW pm	LR pm	R pm	Z pm	pm T	D pm	D pm E
Inverness .... dep	8 20		11t 0					3 40		3 40	3 40	3 40			3 40	
Aberdeen .. .. .. ,,	9 55		12p40	3 40	3 40	5 18		5 18			6 45	7 10			5 30	
Dundee (Tay Bridge)...... ,,	11 50		2p41	5 35	5 35	7 19		7 19		8q 5	8n43	9 7				
,, (West) .. .. ,,	pm		pm												7 10	
Perth (General) .... ,,	12 10		3 27	5 36	5 36	5g36		7 50		7e50	7 50	7 50			8 15	
Glasgow (Central) .. ,,		5 40					9 5		9 25				10 10			
,, (Queen Street) .. ,,	1 0		4 0	6 0	7 30	8 0		8 0		8e 0	8 0	8 0				
,, (St. Enoch) .. ,,														8 50		9 5
Edinburgh (Princes Street) ,,		5 35														
,, (Waverley) .. ,,	2 30		5 14	7 50	8 55	9 35		10 0		10e20	10f40					
	am	am	am	am	am	am	am	am	am	am	am	am	am	am	am	am
LONDON (Euston) .. arr		5d12					6 25		7 0				7 10		7 20	
,, (King's Cross) ,,	3 4		4c45	6 5	5 30	6 20		6 40		6 55	7 15	7 45				
,, (St. Pancras).. ,,														7 20		8 5

WEEKDAYS—*continued*

	D pm	J pm	pm V	DR pm	D pm S
Inverness .... dep		3 40	4 45	5 35	
Aberdeen .. .. .. ,,		5 18			
Dundee (Tay Bridge)...... ,,		7 19			
,, (West) .. .. ,,				8 50	
Perth (General) .... ,,		7 50	8 55	9 45	
Glasgow (Central) .. ,,	10 25				
,, (Queen Street) .. ,,		8 0			
,, (St. Enoch) .. ,,					11 5
Edinburgh (Princes Street) ,,			10E 0		
,, (Waverley) .. ,,		9 50			
	am	am	am	am	am
LONDON (Euston) .. arr	7 35		7 47	8 35	
,, (King's Cross) ,,					
,, (St. Pancras).. ,,		9k 0			10 0

A—Fridays only. Commences 30th June.
a—Morning time.
B—THE ROYAL SCOT.
b—Fridays and Saturdays only. Conveys Buffet Car on Fridays, 16th June to 8th September inclusive, also Restaurant Car on Saturdays.
C—Limited Sleeping accommodation.
c—On Saturdays arrive King's Cross 4.20 am.
D—1st and 3rd class Sleeping accommodation.
d—On Sundays arrives London (Euston) 5.2 am.
E—Except Saturdays.
e—Except on Saturdays, only conveys Sleeping Car passengers from Perth, Glasgow, and Edinburgh. On Saturdays conveys Sleeping Car and ordinary passengers from Edinburgh.
F—THE MID-DAY SCOT.
FO—Fridays only.
f—Only conveys from Edinburgh passengers from North and West of Edinburgh.
G—THE NIGHT SCOTSMAN.
g—Commencing 3rd July departs Perth 7.5 pm.
H—THE FLYING SCOTSMAN.
h—Except Saturday and Sunday nights.
J—1st and 3rd class Sleeping accommodation. Does not convey Sleeping Car passengers from Edinburgh to London.
K—Mondays and Fridays only.
k—On Sunday mornings arrives St. Pancras 8.35 am.
L—THE ABERDONIAN. Limited sleeping accommodation.
M—Will not run on Saturdays, 17th June to 26th August inclusive.
m—Limited Third Class Sleeping accommodation from Edinburgh.
N—Runs on Saturdays, 17th June to 26th August inclusive.
n—Sleeping Car and First Class passengers only.
P—THE THAMES-CLYDE EXPRESS.
p—Afternoon time.
Q—Runs on Saturdays, 17th June to 26th August inclusive. Conveys Through Carriages, Perth to Crewe only, arrive 7.15 pm. Passengers for London (Euston) change at Crewe and arrive Euston 11.11 pm.
q—Limited Sleeping accommodation and Through Carriages to King's Cross except on Saturdays.
R—Restaurant Car whole or part of journey.
r—Departs 12.20 pm on Saturdays.
S—Saturdays only.
T—Fridays only. Runs 30th June to 1st September inclusive.
t—Commencing 1st July departs Inverness 11.20 am.
U—THE QUEEN OF SCOTS. Pullman Cars only. Glasgow to King's Cross. Supplementary charges.
V—Fridays and Saturdays only. Commences 30th June, also Mondays commencing 24th July.
W—Limited Sleeping accommodation, Dundee (Saturdays excepted) and Edinburgh to London (King's Cross).
X—THE CAPITALS LIMITED. NON-STOP, Edinburgh to London (King's Cross).
Y—Saturdays only. Runs until 9th September inclusive.
Z—Sleeping Car train. Conveys sleeping car passengers only.

Heavy figures indicate Through Carriages to London.

A timetable for trains operating between London (Euston) and Glasgow in the 1950s. All these trains would have operated over the TVR. *(Author's Collection)*

Rugby station, immediately after the Second World War. At that time it was in LMS ownership. Ex-LNWR 'Prince of Wales' Class 4–6–0 no. 25802 is resting at the main platform. This engine did not survive into BR ownership. *(A.W.V. Mace Collection)*

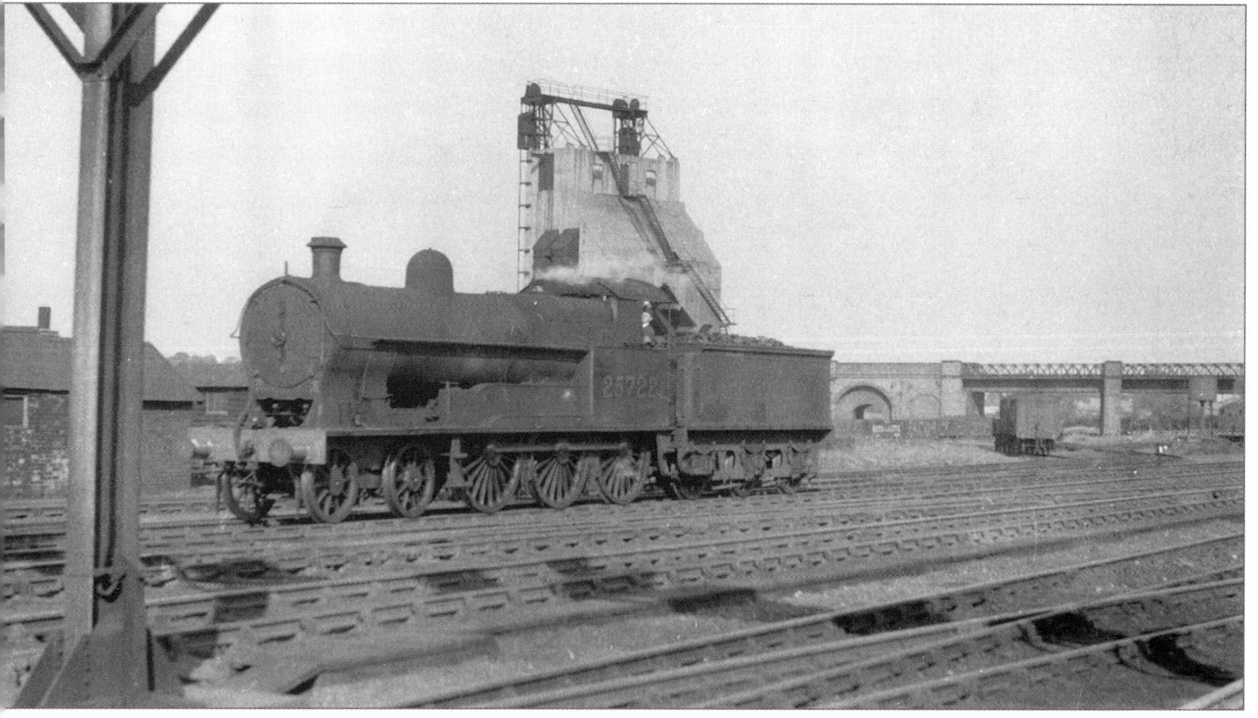

Another view of Rugby in 1945, showing the coaling stage at the locoshed, with an ex-LNWR 'Prince of Wales' Class 4–6–0 at rest. *(A.W.V. Mace Collection)*

Approaching Rugby from London (Euston) at 6.30pm on Sunday 1 July 1951 is ex-LMS 'Princess-Royal' Pacific no. 46210 *Lady Patricia* in the experimental BR blue livery with a northbound train. *(F.W. Shuttleworth Collection)*

A rather dishevelled-looking Rugby station with ex-LNWR 2–4–2 tank locomotive no. 46601 at the head of a local 'Motor Train' for Leamington Spa in the early 1950s. *(R. Carpenter)*

Ex-LMS 'Princess-Coronation' Pacific no. 46237 *City of Bristol* heads a Down express through Rugby as it approaches the TVR in August 1954. To the left is the British Thompson-Houston Company Ltd, an electrical company that was later taken over by electrical giant GEC. The works turned out early electric locomotives for British Railways in the 1960s. To the right is the entrance to Rugby locoshed. *(A.W.V. Mace Collection)*

An ex-LNWR G1 Class 0–8–0 heads an Up freight train past Rugby station in the mid-1950s. *(A.W.V. Mace Collection)*

Another ex-LNWR 0–8–0 freight locomotive heads through Rugby with an engineer's train on 22 July 1956. The complex of lines through Rugby can be appreciated from this view. *(R. Carpenter)*

Ex-LMS rebuilt 'Patriot' Class 4–6–0 no. 45525 *Colwyn Bay* approaches the TVR with a Euston–Blackpool express on 22 July 1956. *(R. Carpenter)*

At the head of Down 'Royal Scot' express is ex-LMS 'Princess-Coronation' Pacific no. 46239 *City of Chester* approaching Rugby station from London (Euston). Following the transfer into BR ownership, the station here was renamed 'Rugby Midland' to avoid confusion with the ex-Great Central/LNER Rugby station which was renamed 'Rugby Central'. *(R. Carpenter)*

Approaching Rugby is ex-LMS 8F 2–8–0 no. 48200 with an Up coal train from Leicester on 23 July 1956. *(R. Carpenter)*

An unidentified express heading towards Rugby from the TVR, *c.* 1958. In addition to the British Thompson-Houston Company, Rugby also had a cement works on the approaches to the TVR and 'Rugby Cement' became a famous product. *(A.W.V. Mace Collection)*

Departing from Rugby on 23 May 1950 with a Liverpool express is ex-LMS rebuilt 'Patriot' Class 4–6–0 no. 45534 *E. Tootal Broadhurst*. Ex-LMS 'Black 5' 4–6–0 no. 44870 is at rest to the right. *(A.W.V. Mace Collection)*

The interior of Rugby Midland station, 1958. An ex-Midland Railway 4P Compound locomotive waits at the head of a stopping train from Euston. This train terminated here. *(A.W.V. Mace Collection)*

BR 'Britannia' Pacific no. 70044 *Earl Haig* departs from Rugby with a northbound express in 1958. These were the first BR locomotives to come into service, from 1951, in an effort to replace the ageing engines of the old railway companies. In the event most of these BR-designed machines had relatively short lives as modern traction took over their role from the late 1950s. *(A.W.V. Mace Collection)*

Awaiting departure from Rugby station in 1959 is ex-LMS 2–6–4 tank locomotive no. 42577 at the head of a local train. *(R. Carpenter)*

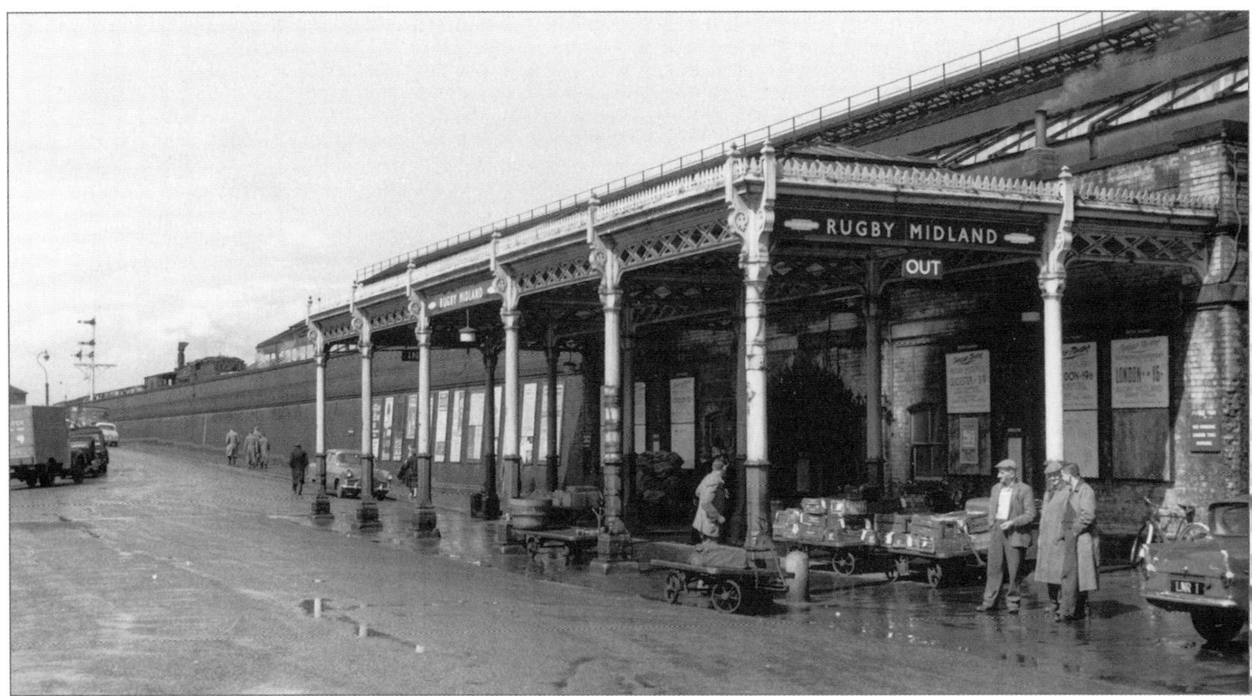

The front entrance to Rugby Midland station as it appeared under BR ownership in 1961. Note the Ford Anglia to the right and the parcels trolleys under the canopy. At that time the railways played a vital role in the movement of goods, but all that would change in the next few years as such traffic was switched to the roads and the railways sank into decline. *(A.W.V. Mace Collection)*

As if to illustrate the previous point, a parcels train, headed by ex-LMS 2–6–0 no. 45704, departing from Rugby on 17 July 1962. These parcels trains would soon be a thing of the past, just like the locomotive that is hauling it, as transport preferences changed. The parcels would soon be going by road and the steam locomotives would be replaced by diesel and electric traction. *(R. Carpenter)*

The ex-LMS 'Jubilee' Class 4–6–0 no. 45583 *Assam* heads a southbound freight past ex-LMS 'Black 5' 4–6–0 on 29 October 1962. *(R. Carpenter)*

The LNWR had a virtual monopoly of train services at Rugby until the Manchester, Sheffield & Lincolnshire Railway decided to build its own route from its, then, southern terminus at Nottingham to London (Marylebone) which was to run via Rugby. The MS&L had been in existence since 1846 and had become a reasonably large organisation but not a prosperous one. Indeed, it had gained the unfortunate nickname 'Money sunk and lost'. The railway company, however, harboured ambitions of reaching London following the appointment of Sir Edward Watkin as general manager in 1853. Having been under the influence of the LNWR, the MS&L now struck out on its own and sought alliance with the Great Northern Railway, instead of harassing the Kings Cross company as it had in the past, and a joint Manchester–Kings Cross service was inaugurated in 1857.

Watkin had, however, resigned from the MS&L. and went to Canada, but in 1863 he returned to the Sheffield company as general manager and was elected to the board as chairman in 1867. He continued trying to take the MS&L to London and sought various partners, but they were all suspicious of him, so he became chairman of the South Eastern Railway in 1866 and of the Metropolitan Railway in 1872. At the same time he became interested in a new company that wished to build a tunnel under the English Channel. Thus Watkin could bring the MS&L down from Nottingham to join up with the Metropolitan Railway, allowing trains to run through London and emerge on the South Eastern Railway, via the East London Railway, and thence to the Channel coast. If the channel tunnel were built, then the MS&L would be able to operate all the way to Paris. As it transpired, there would be no channel tunnel until late into the twentieth century, and a Manchester–Paris express would remain a pipedream.

Despite these thwarted ambitions, Watkin did manage to see through a Parliamentary Bill for the extension of the MS&L, receiving royal assent in 1893. Access to Marylebone was via the Metropolitan Railway. It was this Bill which brought the MS&L into Rugby. The prospect of a line which would compete with the LNWR was welcomed by Rugby businessmen, but they were to be disappointed when the new station in the town was built half a mile away from that of the LNWR. The new route was opened in 1907 and in the same year the MS&L was renamed the Great Central Railway. Here, a Robinson 4–4–0 of the GCR is seen at Rugby station soon after its opening. *(Author's Collection)*

Rugby Central station in BR days. Although the GCR was on the outskirts of Rugby, the new route gave access to the West Riding of Yorkshire, Newcastle upon Tyne, Hull, South Wales, the south-west of England, and the south of England, particularly the port of Southampton, and from its opening the company began tapping Rugby traffic. At the Grouping in 1923, the GCR became a constituent of the LNER despite the fact that its northern section and London line encroached on LMS territory. The LNER found it a useful route between London and the north-east. The 'Central' was added to the station's name following nationalisation in 1948 when the GCR/LNER line became part of British Railways Eastern Region. *(Author's Collection)*

In LNER days, Gresley V2 Class 2–6–2 locomotive no. 889 heads an express made up of Gresley teak carriages through Rugby on its way to Marylebone. *(A.W.V. Mace Collection)*

Again, in LNER days, an Up express passes through Rugby on its way to Marylebone, double-headed by B1 4–6–0 no. 5195 and V2 2–6–2 no. 4820. *(A.W.V. Mace Collection)*

The Down 'South Yorkshireman' passes through Rugby Central headed by Gresley A3 Pacific no. 60107 *Royal Lancer* in the early BR days. *(A.W.V. Mace Collection)*

Leaving Rugby Central at the head of a Down stopping train in the early 1950s is ex-GCR J11 Class 0–6–0 no. 64313. *(A.W.V. Mace Collection)*

Entering Rugby Central station in the late 1950s is BR Class 9F 2–10–0 no. 92011 at the head of a southbound mineral train. Empty coal wagons wait in the sidings within the station confines. *(A.W.V. Mace Collection)*

Ex-LNER B1 Class 4–6–0 no. 61177 heads a Leicester–south coast excursion through Rugby in the late 1950s. Only a decade later this whole line would be closed. The GCR had been the last of the major trunk routes to London and, from its inception in 1899, was the most expendable. Indeed, under proposals made by the infamous Dr Beeching in his 'Reshaping Report' of 1963, the whole of the GCR, from its border with London Transport at Aylesbury to the outskirts of Sheffield, including Rugby, was closed completely by May 1969. *(A.W.V. Mace Collection)*

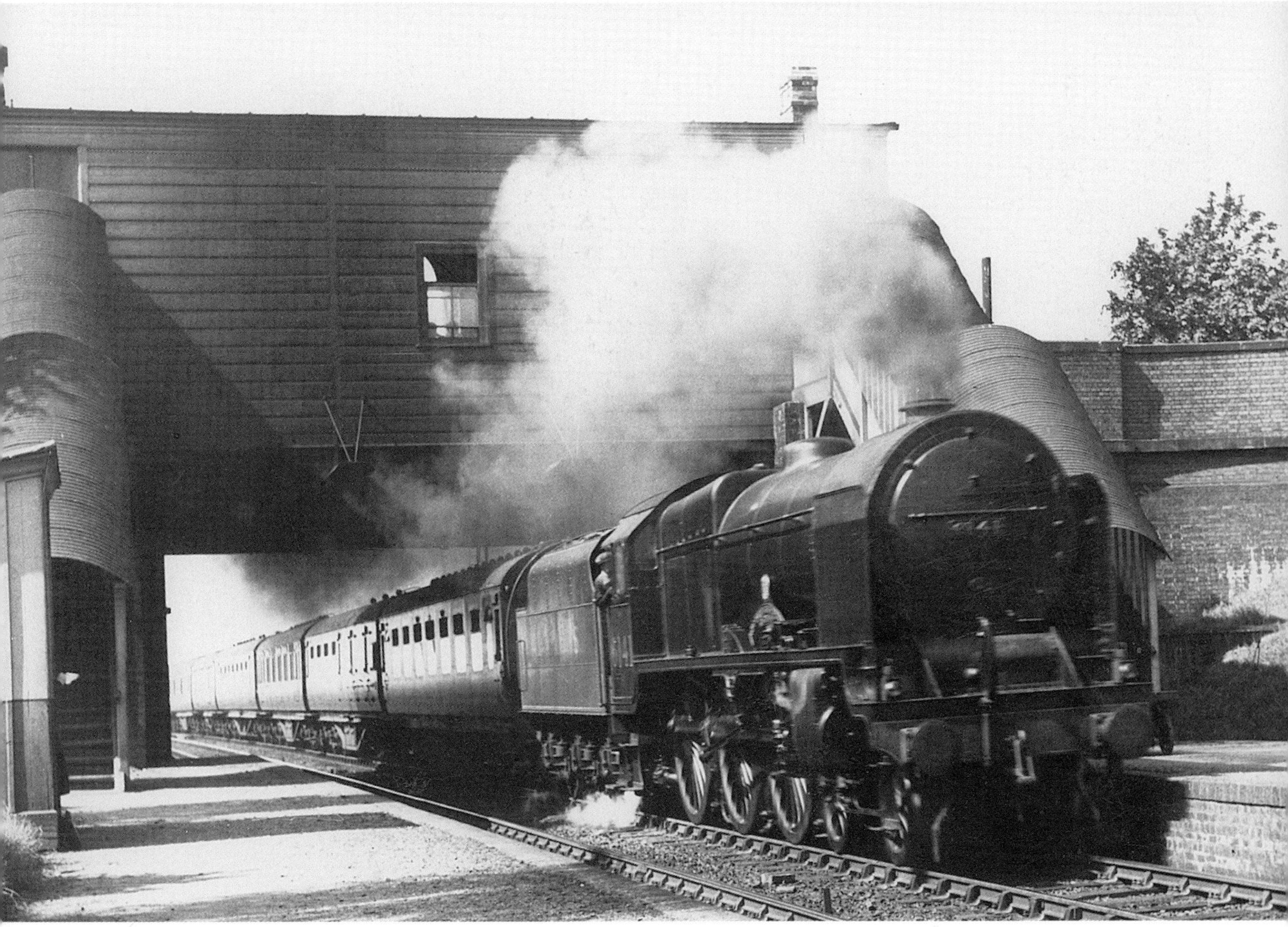

Some 5½ miles from Rugby is the first station on the TVR at Brinklow, seen here in 1932 with LMS 'Royal-Scot' 4–6–0 no. 6141 *The North Staffordshire Regiment* at the head of a southbound express. Brinklow station was opened on 1 December 1847 and was originally named Stretton. The name was changed to Brinklow from 1 February 1870. The station seen here is not the original, which was some 2 miles further north. It served the little village of Brinklow, about half a mile away, which was the birthplace of the fifteenth-century writer Sir Thomas Malory. Brinklow station possessed only a modest and plain station building, which had its frontage on the road that crossed the railway at the northern end. This road is actually the Fosse Way, a Roman road linking Bath and Lincoln. The front and side walls of the station building were constructed of brick and straddled the running lines. The legend 'BRINKLOW STATION' was carved into panels above the windows flanking the central entrance. The rear wall was of timber, while steps down to the platforms were roofed in corrugated iron. The station had a small goods yard on the Up side, which could accommodate 38 wagons. A further 25 wagons could be stabled in the dead-end of the Down slow line. As the TVR quickly became crowded with trains, it was widened in several places between 1871 and 1910. The first section so treated was between Rugby and Bulkington, an Up slow line being opened on 14 August 1871. While this three-track section sufficed for some years, traffic increases forced the LNWR to seek further widening of the 13½ miles between Rugby and Nuneaton. Under an Act of 1899, authority was given for this work. However, other than the sections between Rugby and Brinklow and between Attleborough sidings and Nuneaton the work was never carried out. Brinklow station was closed on 14 September 1957 but freight services here survived until 20 February 1961. *(G. Coltas)*

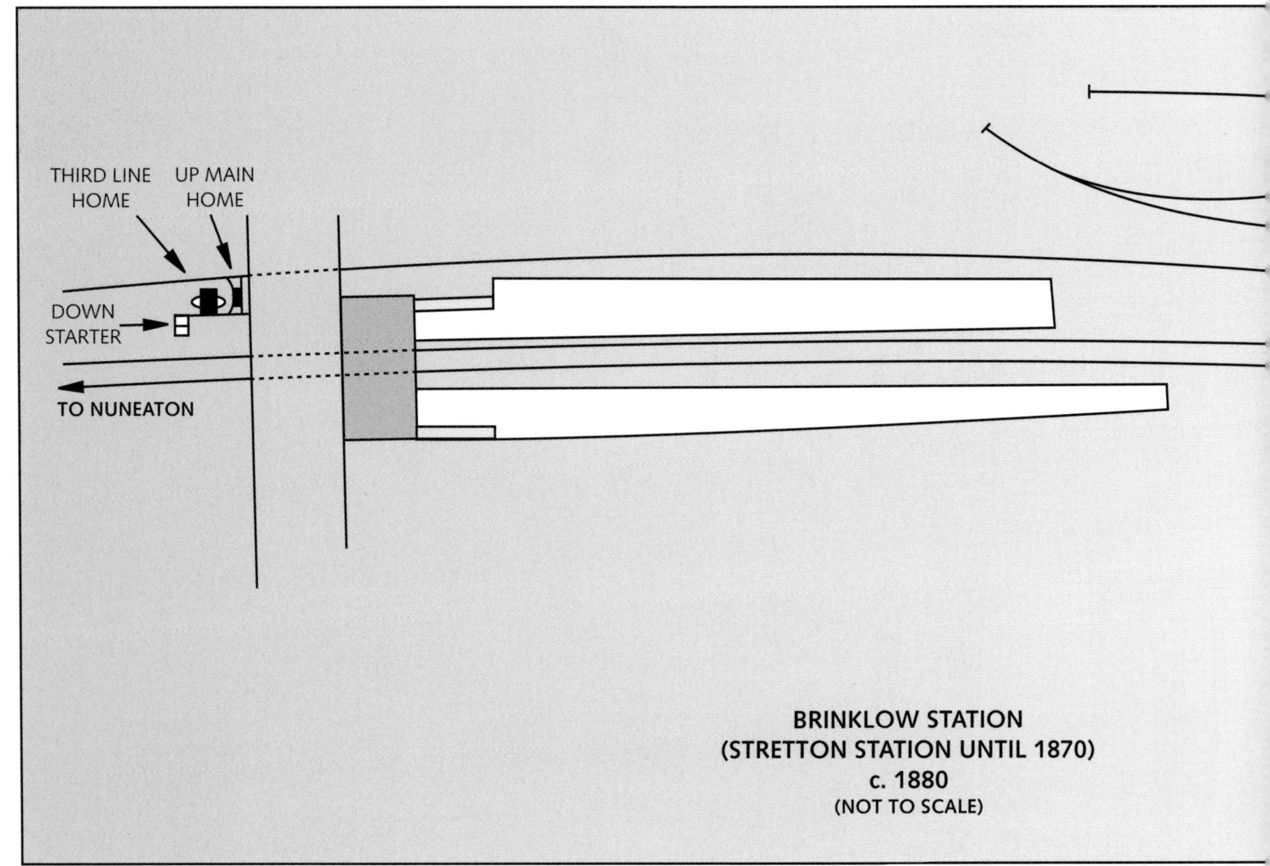

Opposite: A general view of Shilton station from the overbridge in LMS days. Note the waiting shelter on the Down platform and the goods siding beyond the Up platform, with GWR, LMS, GN, NE, and various privately owned wagons. Shilton was another TVR station which opened on 1 December 1847. It served a small community where a cottage industry in ribbon making had existed for many years. As at Brinklow, the station building was constructed of brick at the front and sides, with a timber rear; it straddled the running lines. The station name was carved on tablets above the window frames facing a road which crossed the railway at its northern end. In 1876 the only siding accommodation at Shilton was a Down refuge siding just north of the station, and there were no ordinary goods facilities. This deficiency was rectified in 1880, when a single siding was laid into the Up third line (opened in 1871). This new siding, which was controlled from a small cabin on the Down platform, was about 350 feet in length and was capable of holding 22 wagons, although in LMS days the capacity was given as 14. In September 1898 the Down refuge siding was extended back through the station and converted into a goods loop. The old cabin was removed and two new signal-boxes were erected on the Up side. Station cabin no. 1 contained 14 levers, while no. 2 box, 1,029 yards to the north, contained 11. Originally, no. 2 box signalled all the running lines, but in LMS days its control over the Up line ceased. Shilton no. 2 box closed in the early 1950s, and the loop platform line to the Down crossover was removed, the whole Down goods loop being worked by the former no. 1 box. *(Author's Collection)*

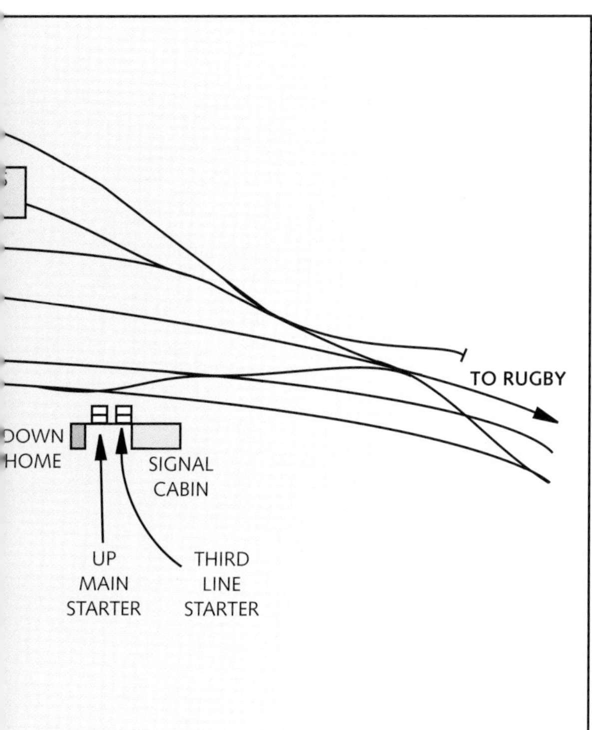

A plan of Brinklow station showing the situation of the main buildings and the goods sidings. *(Author)*

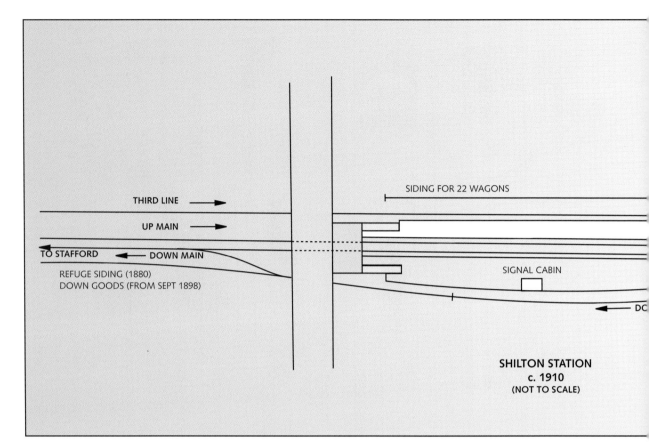

SIDING FOR 22 WAGONS
THIRD LINE
UP MAIN
TO STAFFORD
DOWN MAIN
REFUGE SIDING (1880)
DOWN GOODS (FROM SEPT 1898)
SIGNAL CABIN
DC

SHILTON STATION
c. 1910
(NOT TO SCALE)

A view of Shilton station showing the Up siding and main station building in LNWR days. Over the years the timber backing to the main station building was patched up and became rather shabby. The stairways to each platform were covered by arched corrugated iron, all of which combined to make the approach look rather tatty. *(Author's Collection)*

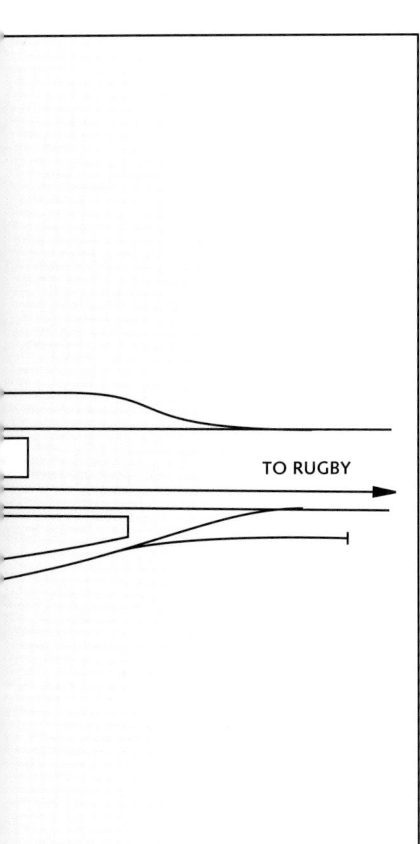

Shilton station plan showing the layout of the goods lines and the station buildings. *(Author)*

A closer view of the main building at Shilton station in LNWR days, well before all the patching took place. Like Brinklow, Shilton station was closed to passengers on 14 September 1957, but it remained open to freight traffic until 1965. *(Author's Collection)*

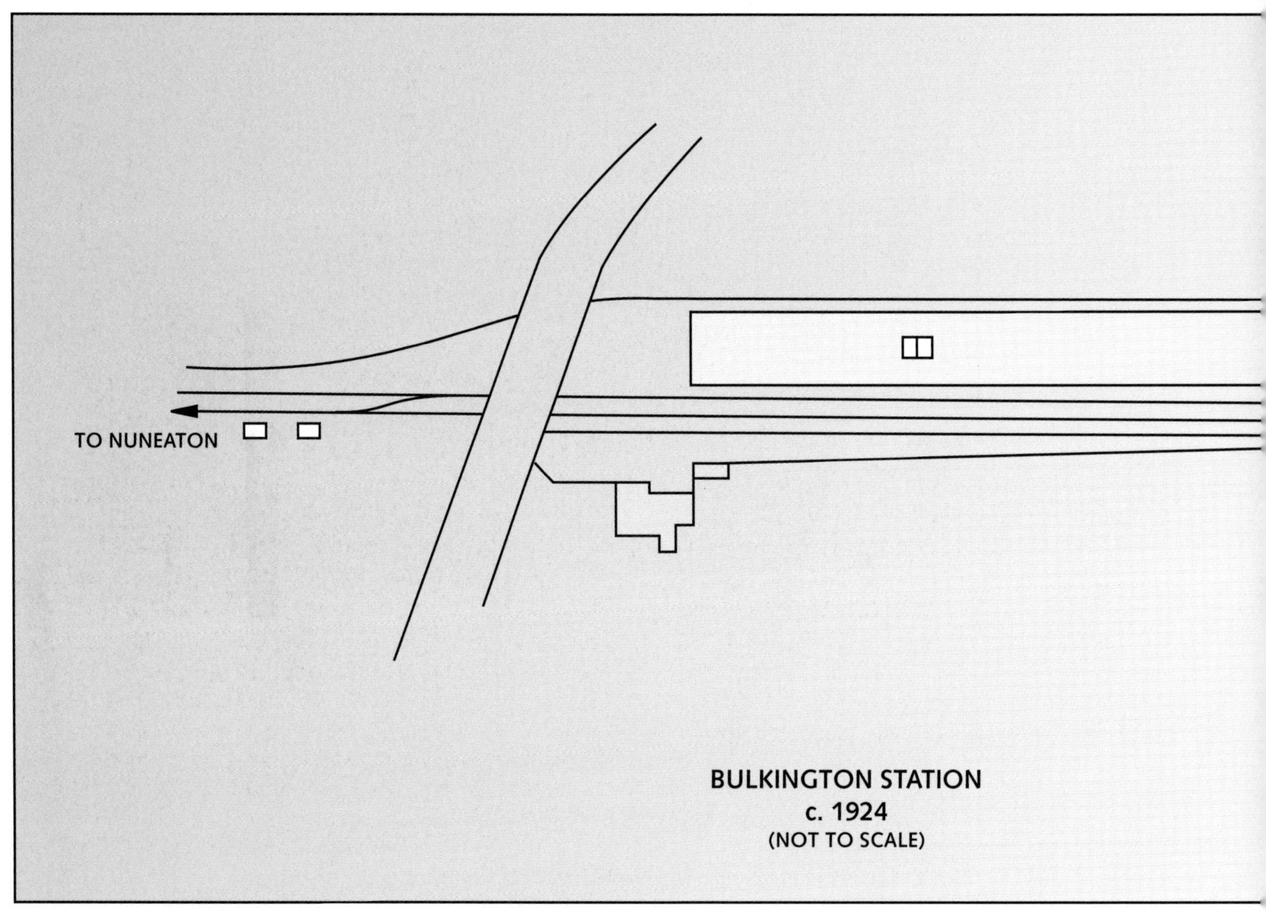

A plan of the small and short-lived Bulkington station. *(Author)*

Opposite: Before the railways were nationalised in 1948, the LMS embarked on an experiment in diesel-electric traction, following the company's success with diesel shunters in the 1930s, when H.A. Ivatt, the chief mechanical engineer at Derby, worked in conjunction with the English-Electric Company to produce two 1–C–C–1 locomotives, which proved to be the forerunners of today's main-line diesels. The first, no. 10000, emerged from Derby works in the first week of December 1947, only a month before nationalisation, giving the company time to have its LMS legend carried on the new engine. The second locomotive, no. 10001, emerged early in 1948 as a BR machine. These two engines often worked double-headed on the TVR. Here no. 10001 is seen at the head of a Down Blackpool service near Bulkington on 12 July 1952. The TVR also saw Southern Region diesel-electric locomotive no. 10202 on the 'Royal-Scot' service during 1952, this being one of three built at Ashford. *(Author's Collection)*

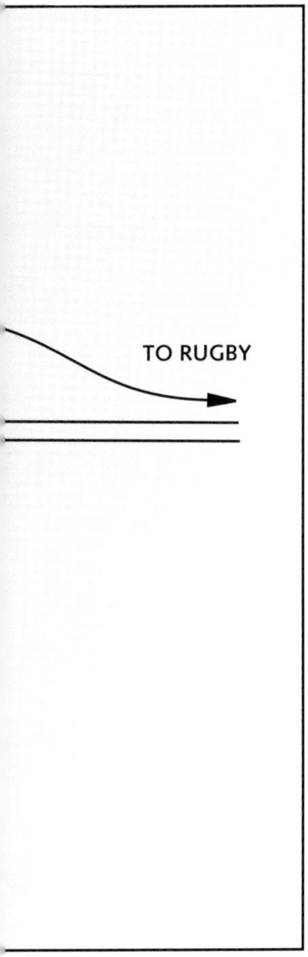

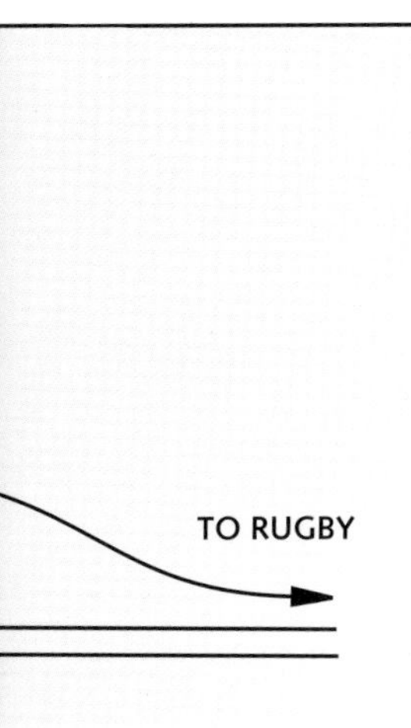

Just 2½ miles beyond Shilton was Bulkington station, seen here in 1962. The Jacobean-style main building, on the Down side, remains *in situ* as a private house. When it opened on 1 December 1847, the station was provided with two through lines and an Up side loop to an island platform. Access to the station was via steps from a road overbridge at the northern end. The station was controlled from a Saxby & Farmer signal cabin, erected between the road overbridge and the main station building in 1873. Its signal frame was renewed in 1911. Bulkington station was closed as an economy measure, owing to the effects of the Great Depression on revenue for the LMS, on 18 May 1931, and never reopened. *(R. Carpenter)*

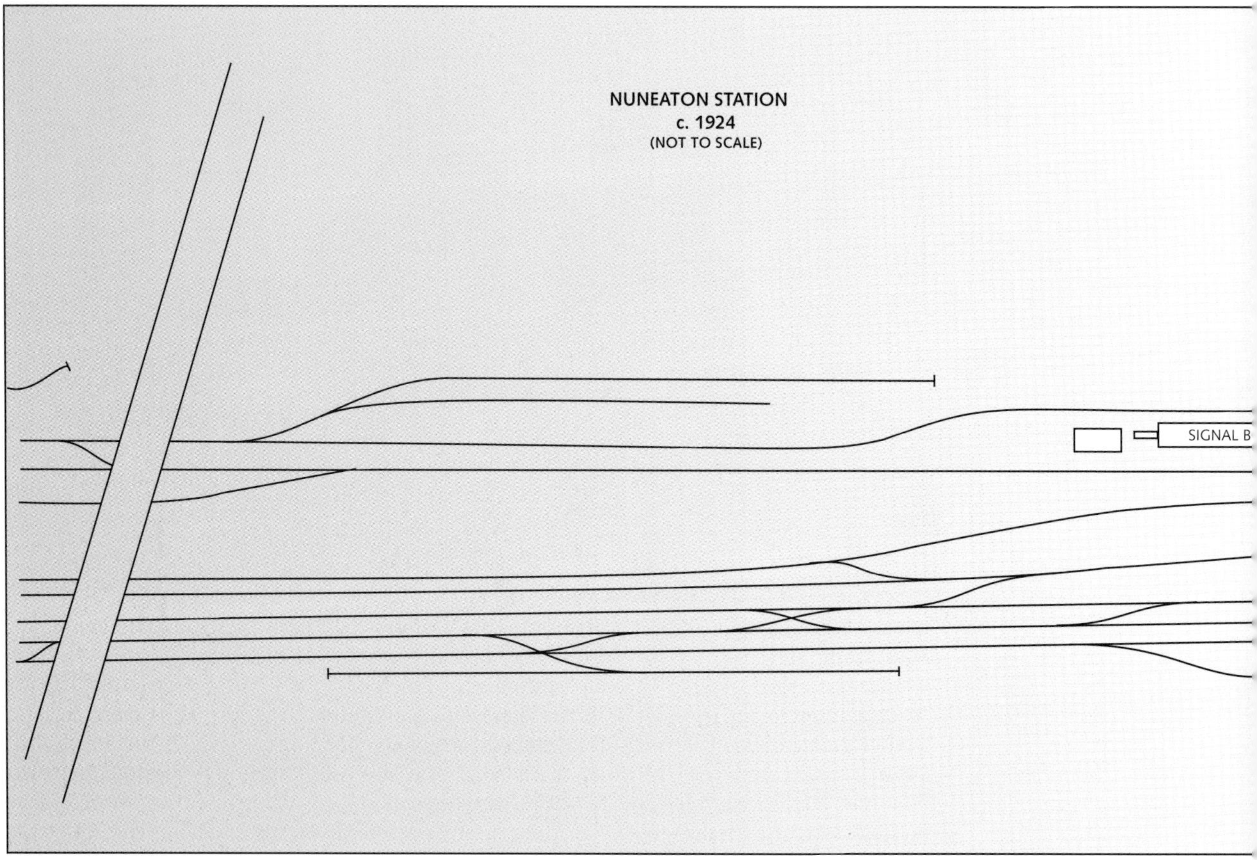

The southern end of Nuneaton station in the mid-1920s. *(Author)*

An unidentified ex-LMS 'Black 5' 4–6–0 passing Attleborough, south of Nuneaton, in June 1953 with an Up special train. Near here was Bedworth Colliery which, with other local mines, provided much freight traffic for the TVR, producing much revenue for the railway companies. Also in the same area there was stone quarrying for Cambrian rock, a close-grained granite. *(Author's Collection)*

Opposite: Ex-LMS 'Jubilee' Class 4–6–0 no. 45644 *Howe* heading the Up 'Mancunian' out of Nuneaton on 28 February 1953. The branch to Leicester can be seen in the background on the right. *(Author's Collection)*

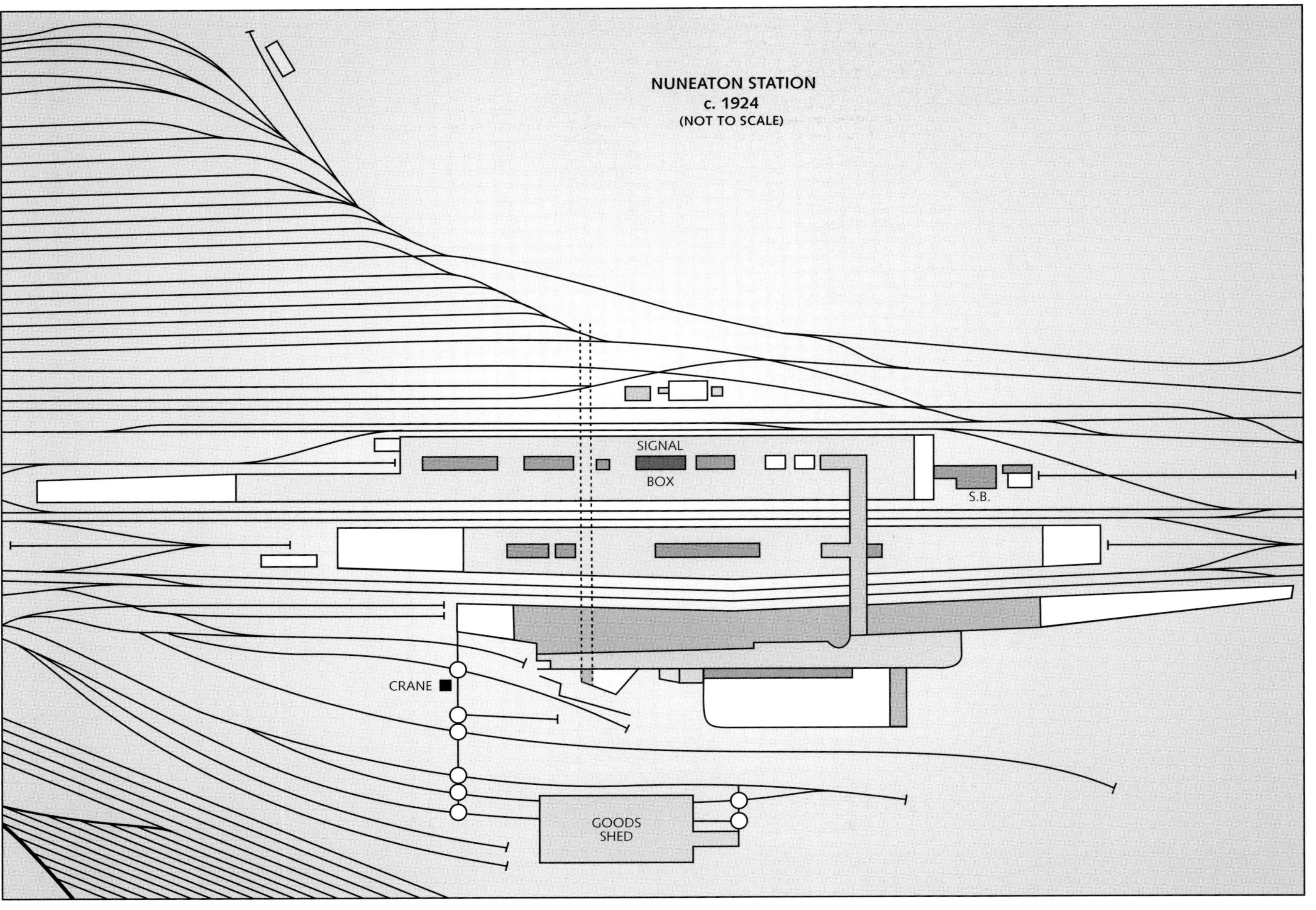
NUNEATON STATION
c. 1924
(NOT TO SCALE)
SIGNAL
BOX
S.B.
CRANE
GOODS
SHED

The Up 'Merseyside Express', headed by ex-LMS 'Princess-Royal' Pacific no. 46205 *Princess Victoria*, approaching Nuneaton from the north and passing Ashby Junction on 11 September 1954. The station was to become, perhaps, the most important on the TVR. Nuneaton (meaning the river town of the Nuns) is approached after the TVR crosses the River Anker, a mile to the south, and its priory church of St Mary was built in Norman times. Since those far-off days industry has taken over and Nuneaton became a centre for collieries, brick and tile industries and drainpipe manufacture, the latter two drawing their raw materials from local marls. The town has also manufactured hats, ready-made clothing and ribbon, as well as being involved in tapestry weaving, plush making, worsted spinning, the production of elastics, webbing, needles and sports equipment, fellmongering, leather dressing, dyeing, along with box and wooden heel making. Little wonder then that the railway and station at Nuneaton expanded so rapidly from inauspicious beginnings when the TVR was opened. Over the years the Trent Valley station at Nuneaton grew apace, and the railway became increasingly complex, with the development of substantial sidings flanking both sides of the station to cater for the freight traffic demand. *(R. Carpenter)*

Opposite: A plan of the station at Nuneaton, showing the main buildings, goods shed and substantial sidings. It all shows what an important station Nuneaton had become on the TVR. At the bottom left is the entrance to the substantial carriage sidings. *(Author)*

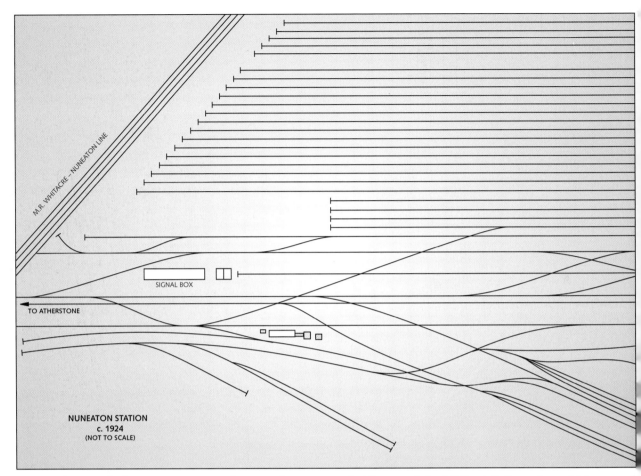

M.R. WHITACRE – NUNEATON LINE

SIGNAL BOX

TO ATHERSTONE

NUNEATON STATION
c. 1924
(NOT TO SCALE)

The northern end of Nuneaton station showing the expanse of sidings and the Midland Railway line which crossed the TVR here. *(Author)*

When it opened the station at Nuneaton was given only 'Second Class' status, but it was to grow into the largest of five junctions that developed on the TVR, receiving a line from Coventry in 1850 and additional lines from Hinckley in 1862, Leicester in 1864 and Moira in 1873. The prime reason for the later importance of Nuneaton was the fact that it was the only intermediate town (and the only one with rail junctions lying on a direct route) projected by the Midland Railway between Birmingham and Leicester. The MR station was at Abbey Street, its line crossing the TVR just north of the Trent Valley station. Access to the LNWR was via a loop line at Ashby Junction, a joint venture by the two companies, which opened in 1880. In 1873 the two companies also opened a joint line from Nuneaton to Burton-on-Trent and Coalville, starting from Ashby Junction. From the 1880s Anglo-Scottish expresses made a stop at Nuneaton, which enhanced the status of the station, raising it from a 'Second Class' stopping place to a 'First Class' station. Given that Nuneaton had become an important junction, it is rather surprising that the TVR station had such a minor role for so long. Unlike other 'First Class' stations, Nuneaton did not have any refreshment facilities until 1881, when a refreshment room was opened, although it did not provide hot lunches for travellers. Like other stations where Anglo-Scottish expresses called, Nuneaton provided luncheon baskets for passengers. Costing 3*s*, these baskets contained either half a chicken with ham or tongue, or a portion of cold beef, and salad, ice, bread, cheese and butter; and either a half bottle of claret, two glasses of sherry or a pint bottle of stout. As Nuneaton's status grew, the station was enlarged and it was partly rebuilt in 1913. Reconstruction of the Down platform and main station building was given to a local contractor from nearby Foleshill, at a cost of £31,822 5*s* 5*d*. The architect designed a plain, simple building with a small clock tower at the London end. Small circular windows were provided in the centre portion of the upper floor. The overall impression was one of simple elegance which still gave the building a modern appearance some fifty years after completion. The updating of Nuneaton station was not completed until 1915, when its importance as a refreshment stop for West Coast expresses was further enhanced with the opening of new dining rooms, which provided breakfasts, luncheons, teas, dinners and light refreshments. It is this completed station which can be seen in this view in LNWR days. *(Author's Collection)*

Opposite: Passing through Nuneaton are ex-LMS 'Black 5' 4–6–0s nos 44684 and 45193 on a Down relief Manchester train on 8 August 1953. Approaching Nuneaton from Bulkington, the TVR runs past Dorlcote Mill (some 3 miles away), near the home of author Mary Ann Evans, better known as George Eliot. Her book *The Mill on the Floss* was based on Dorlcote Mill. *(Author's Collection)*

L. & N. W. R.

The following

HOTELS

Are under the Company's Management.

LONDON (Euston) ... ... Euston Hotel.
Tel. No.: Museum 3000. Telegraphic Address: "Bestotel, Eusquare, London."

BIRMINGHAM (New Street Station) ... Queen's Hotel.
Tel. No.: Central 5531. Telegraphic Address: "Bestotel, Birmingham."

LIVERPOOL (Lime Street) ... North Western Hotel.
Tel No.: Royal 2960. Telegraphic Address: "Bestotel, Liverpool."

BLETCHLEY ... ... Station Hotel.
Telegraphic Address: "Bestotel, Bletchley"

CREWE ... ... Crewe Arms Hotel.
Tel No.: 21. Telegraphic Address: "Bestotel, Crewe."

HOLYHEAD ... ... Station Hotel.
Tel. No.: 24. Telegraphic Address: "Bestotel, Holyhead."

GREENORE ... ... Greenore Hotel.
Telegraphic Address: "Bestotel, Greenore."

PRESTON (L. & Y. and L. & N. W. R.) ... Park Hotel.
Tel. No.: 188. Telegraphic Address: "Bestotel, Preston."

DUBLIN (North Wall) ... ... North Western Hotel.
Tel. No.: 1291. Telegraphic Address. "Northwestern Hotel, Dublin."

Hotel Porters in Red Coats meet the Trains and Boats and convey visitors' luggage free to and from the Hotels.

Telegrams ordering rooms at the above Hotels will be sent free of charge from any Station on the North Western or Caledonian Systems on notice being given to a Station Official or to the Guard of the Train by which the intending Visitor is travelling.

New Dining Rooms

AT

EUSTON and NUNEATON STATIONS.

Very comfortable and handsomely appointed **Dining Rooms** have been opened, and **Breakfasts, Luncheons, Teas, Dinners,** and **Light Refreshments** can be obtained at reasonable prices.

Hot Luncheons, Table d'Hôte or à la Carte, from 12.30 to 2.30 p.m.

EUSTON STATION,
LONDON, N.W.

GUY CALTHROP,
General Manager.

The LNWR wasted no time in publicising the fact that such 'handsomely appointed' dining facilities were available at Nuneaton, as this 1915 advert shows. *(Author's Collection)*

The LMS had become interested in alternatives to steam traction in the 1930s and had been successful in using diesel engines in its shunting locomotives. It also took an interest in English Electric's experimental diesel-electric railcar, seen here on a local service at Nuneaton station on 12 May 1937. During the Depression years the railways were urgently seeking cheaper alternatives to steam engines. *(Author's Collection)*

Above: Ex-LNWR 'Prince of Wales' Class 4–6–0 as LMS no. 25648 *Queen of the Belgians* is seen resting at Nuneaton station in 1947. The LNWR became part of the London Midland & Scottish Railway in 1923 when all the railway companies were grouped into four large undertakings following the success of government control during the First World War. While most railway employees would have preferred to see a nationalised railway, the government of the day was not so keen and under the Railway Act of 1921, the 120 railway companies were grouped into just four, the change taking effect from 1 January 1923. It would not be until 1 January 1948, after the intervention of the Second World War, that the railways would come under state ownership. *(H.F. Wheeler Collection)*

Table 12

THE LAKES EXPRESS

THROUGH RESTAURANT CAR EXPRESS TRAIN

BETWEEN

LONDON AND THE LAKE DISTRICT

WEEKDAYS

		noon	
London (Euston)	dep	12 0	
		pm	
Wigan (North Western)	arr	3 53	
	dep	3 57	
Preston	arr	4 22	
	dep	4 26	
Lancaster (Castle)	arr	4 55	
	dep	4 57	
Oxenholme	arr	5 22	
	dep	5 27	5 35
Kendal	arr	..	5 39
Burneside	,,	....	5 46
Staveley	,,	..	5 55
Windermere¶	,,	....	6 5
Penrith*	arr	6 16	..
Blencow	,,	6 34	....
Penruddock	,,	6 43	..
Troutbeck†	,,	6 48	....
Threlkeld	,,	6 56	..
Keswick	,,	7 5	....
Braithwaite	,,	7 31	..
Bassenthwaite Lake	,,	7 40	....
Embleton	,,	7 46	..
Cockermouth‡	,,	7 52	....
Brigham	,,	7 59	..
Camerton	,,	8 6	....
Workington Bridge	,,	8 15	..
Workington (Main)	,,	8 20	....

		am	am
Workington (Main)	dep	8 35	....
Brigham	,,	8 54	..
Cockermouth‡	,,	9 2	....
Bassenthwaite Lake	,,	9 13	..
Braithwaite	,,	9 21	....
Keswick	,,	9 38	..
Penrith*	,,	10 24	....
Tebay	,,	11 0	..
Windermere¶	dep	....	10 50
Staveley	,,	..	10 59
Burneside	,,	.....	11 4
Kendal	,,	..	11 13
Oxenholme	arr	11 17	11 19
	dep	11 30	
Carnforth	arr	11 46	
	dep	11 50	
		pm	
Lancaster	arr	12 0	
	dep	12 5	
Preston	arr	12 35	
		SX	SO
		pm	pm
	dep	12 45	12 43
Wigan (North Western)	arr	1 11	—
	dep	1 16	—
Warrington (Bank Quay)	arr	1 38	—
	dep	1 43	—
Crewe	arr	2 15	1 58
	dep	2 24	2 8
London (Euston)	arr	5 21	5 9

NOTES

SO—Saturdays only.
SX—Saturdays excepted.

*—Station for Ullswater Lake (Pooley Bridge) (5¾ miles).
†—Station for Ullswater Lake (5¾ miles).
‡—Station for Buttermere.
¶—Station for Bowness (1¼ miles) and Ambleside (4¼ miles).

Restaurant Car and Through Carriages between London and Windermere. Through Carriages between London and Workington via Keswick.

Seats on these trains are reservable in advance for passengers travelling from London (Euston), Windermere and Workington (Main) on payment of fee of 1/- per seat.

An advertisement for the 'Lakes Express', another express service that ran along the TVR. The 'Lakes Express' started from Euston and travelled to resorts in the Cumbrian Lake District, a favourite destination for hillwalkers and holidaymakers. *(Author's Collection)*

Ex-LMS 'Royal-Scot' Class 4–6–0 no. 46111 *Royal Fusilier*, about to depart from Nuneaton on 27 March 1954 with the 8.30am Euston–Liverpool (Lime Street) train. *(Author's Collection)*

Resting at Nuneaton is ex-LNWR 0–8–0 freight engine no. 49181 with an engineer's train during May 1952. These locomotives were a common sight on the TVR at the head of heavy freight trains during steam days and their success in this role ensured a long life for these engines. They were introduced by the LNWR in 1920. *(R. Carpenter)*

Ex-LMS 'Princess-Coronation' Pacific no. 46249 *City of Sheffield* enters Nuneaton at the head of an express bound for Euston. Situated on the main line between Euston and the north, the TVR saw all the top-link express engines of the LNWR/LMS/BR at the head of important express trains. *(R. Carpenter)*

Ex-LMS 'Jubilee' Class 4–6–0 no. 45584 *North-West Frontier* approaches Nuneaton at the head of an express train on 11 September 1954. *(H.F. Wheeller Collection)*

Coming out of Abbey Junction, where the LNWR met the MR at Abbey Street, and joining the TVR at Weddington Junction, are ex-LMS '8F' 2–8–0 no. 48657 and Hughes Class 5F 2–6–0 no. 42885. *(H.F. Wheeller Collection)*

Another view of Abbey Junction, with ex-LMS 4F 0–6–0 no. 44103 at the head of a goods train passing ex-LNWR 8F 0–8–0 no. 49342 on its way to join the TVR. *(H.F. Wheeller Collection)*

Ex-Midland Railway 3F 0–6–0 at the head of a local train at Abbey Street station on 14 April 1957. It was this station that was linked to the Trent Valley Railway by Ashby Junction. The MR had opened its line between Nuneaton and Leicester in 1864. Along with several others, the MR line enabled the railway network in the town to grow at a rapid rate, and this was probably one of the reasons why Anglo-Scottish expresses and other trains to the north stopped at Nuneaton, in order to make connections with trains from these other lines, thereby allowing, for example, the booking of tickets to Glasgow from Leicester. *(H.C. Casserley)*

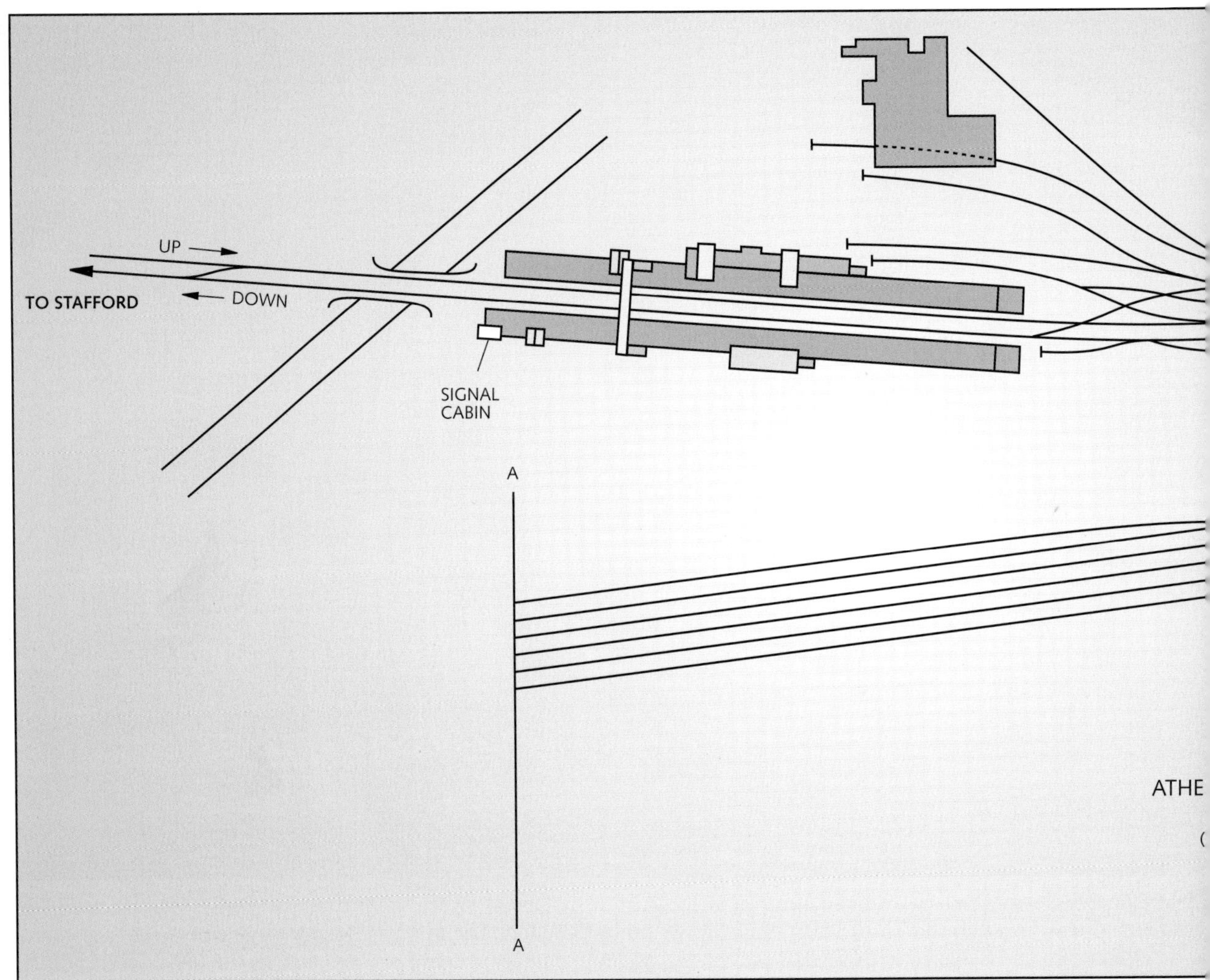

Opposite: The 'Irish Mail' passing through Atherstone station. This photograph was taken before the line here wa quadrupled, and shows the station featured in the plan above. Opened on 15 September 1847 it was one of the 'Firs Class' stations, with its main building designed in the Jacobean style. The town itself was a centre for hat making which was a cottage industry for many years until factory production took over. Under the LNWR (Additional Powers Act 1892, permission was given to quadruple the TVR between Tamworth and a point just north of Atherstone leve crossing. The A5 Holyhead Road crossed the TVR at this point, and had been a source of conflict betwee Warwickshire County Council and the LNWR for some years. In 1898–9 the council had obtained an injunctio against the LNWR which banned the railway company from running trains over the road at more tha 4 mph. The Tamworth–Atherstone quadrupling was brought into use on 1 July 1901. Powers for the quadrupling c the Atherstone–Nuneaton section were obtained in the LNWR Act of 1902. This Act also authorised the LNWR t divert Watling Street (the A5) over the railway and Coventry Canal by means of a bridge, and to close the contentiou level crossing. This latter task was completed in September 1903. *(Author's Collection)*

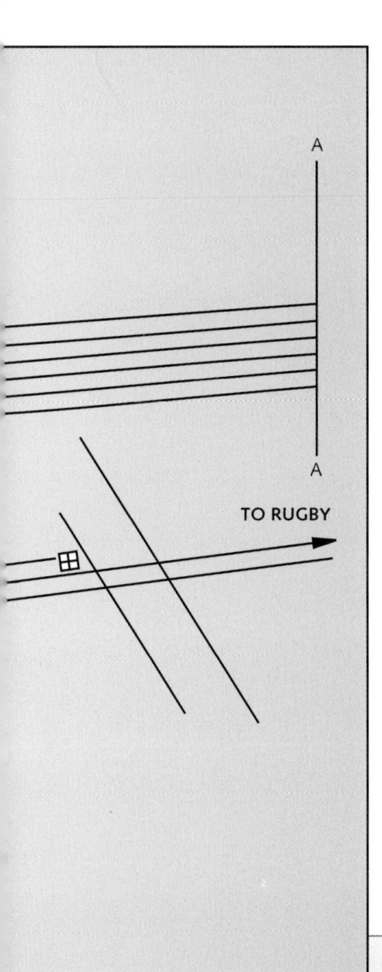

A plan of Atherstone station as it appeared in about 1887 before the TVR in this area was quadrupled. *(Author)*

Atherstone station shortly after the line was quadrupled. The 'First Class' station had its interior layout altered and modernised when the quadrupled line from Tamworth was opened. The Jacobean frontage was not greatly affected at this time but a few years later the original chimneys on the residential side of the building were replaced by smaller, more modern ones. Quadrupling also brought changes to the station itself. The old Down platform was removed, along with the original signal-box. A timber building was erected on the Down platform, and a new replacement signal-box was centrally situated and carried on girders, one set of supports being placed on the new Down platform, the others being on the slightly enlarged 'six-foot' between the fast lines. Access to the new box was via a catwalk from the Down side. The new signal-box had an extended roof and bargeboards typical of post-1904 LNWR boxes, but with shallow windows of earlier design. This new signal-box can be clearly seen in this view. An unusual aspect of the station itself was the short awning on the Up side. The awning supports were placed, rather inconveniently, very close together and were somewhat less than the regulation 6ft from the platform edge. Between Atherstone and Polesworth the Baddesley Colliery Company had substantial mine workings and its branch line, which crossed the A5 on the level, ran from Baddesley pit head to the TVR near Atherstone. This line was operated by one of only four Garrett engines ever built for British industrial railways. *(Author's Collection)*

Opposite, top: On 22 July 1947 there was an accident at Polesworth involving streamlined 'Princess-Coronation' Pacific no. 6244 *King George VI* on the Down Euston–Liverpool express. The run-down state of the British railway system following intensive use during the Second World War was such that accidents like this were not uncommon at the time. Another possible cause could have been subsidence, given that Baddesley Colliery had substantial mineworkings in the area, some of which passed under the TVR. Indeed the problem was so serious that in the 1930s the LMS was involved in litigation resulting from mining subsidence at Polesworth. To overcome these problems, the railway company bought up all the mineral rights beneath the TVR and had the line restored for high-speed running. *(R. Carpenter)*

Another accident at Polesworth involving an unidentified 'Princess-Coronation' Pacific on 19 November 1951, in early BR days. The Jacobean-style Polesworth station can be seen in the background. *(R. Carpenter)*

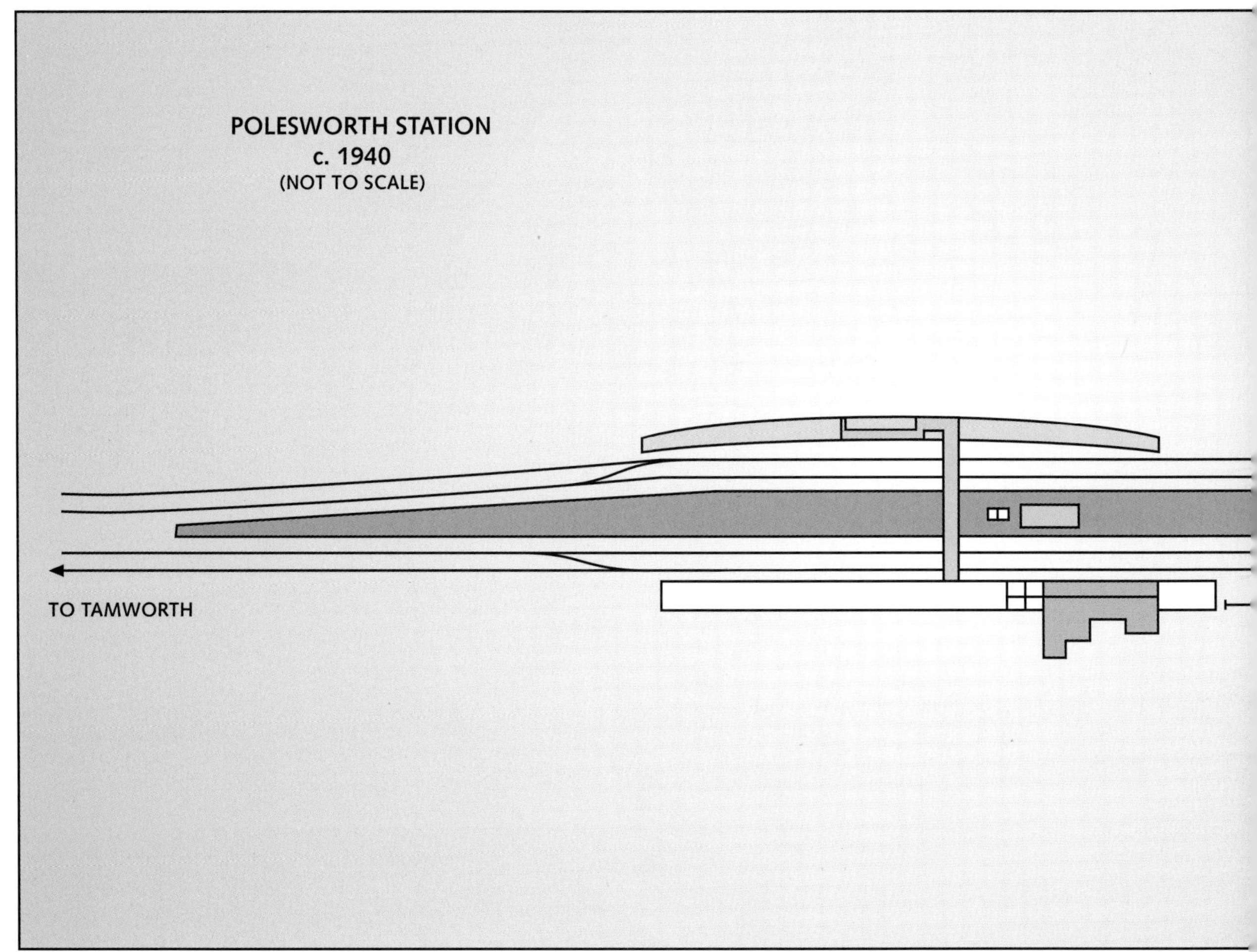

Opposite: Resting at Tamworth station in LNWR days is 'Jumbo' 2–4–0 no. 2194 *Cambrian*, waiting at the head of a Down semi-fast train. Tamworth was an important station on the TVR from the day it opened on 15 September 1847. It was a 'First Class' station from the start, being a mail interchange point, the Midland Railway's Birmingham & Derby Junction line actually arrived in the town first, being opened on 12 August 1839, and its route crossed the TVR here. Midland Railway trains operated between Lincoln, Birmingham, Bristol and York, and mail for the north-west and Scotland from these towns was exchanged at Tamworth. The buildings at the TVR station reflected the importance of Tamworth to the TVR. At the Polesworth end the Up platform had a single-storey building while the main building on the Down platform was a two-storey structure in the usual TVR Jacobean style. The High Level (MR) and Low Level (TVR) stations were at right angles to each other and were connected with lifts for mail interchange, and by a sharply curved spur for transferring vehicles. The TVR runs at right angles to, and passes underneath, the MR station under a bridge. A chord line from the LNWR to the MR was completed in June 1847. New Tamworth stations were opened on 24 September 1962, where efficient mail interchange facilities were major factors in their design. The TVR station was worked by two signal-boxes, nos 1 and 2 in mechanical days, but with the introduction of MAS signalling this was reduced to one box (the former no. 2). *(R. Carpenter)*

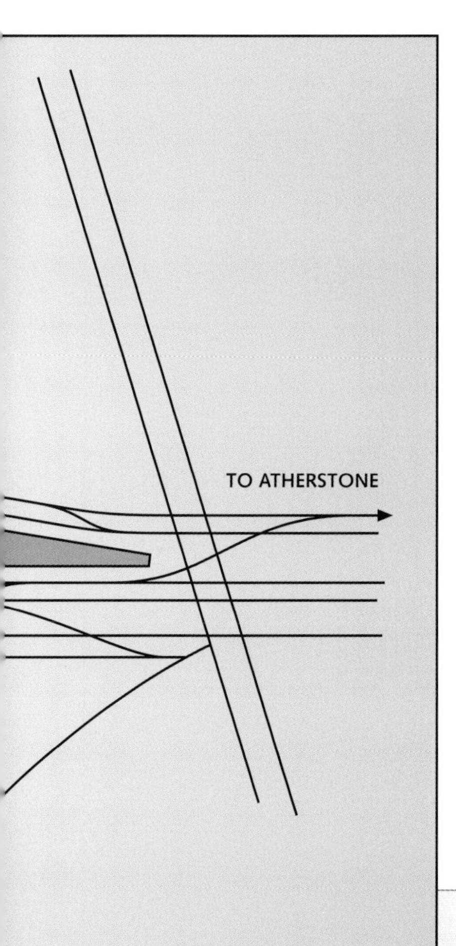

A plan of Polesworth station in the 1940s. The main station building was at the Atherstone end of the platform. *(Author)*

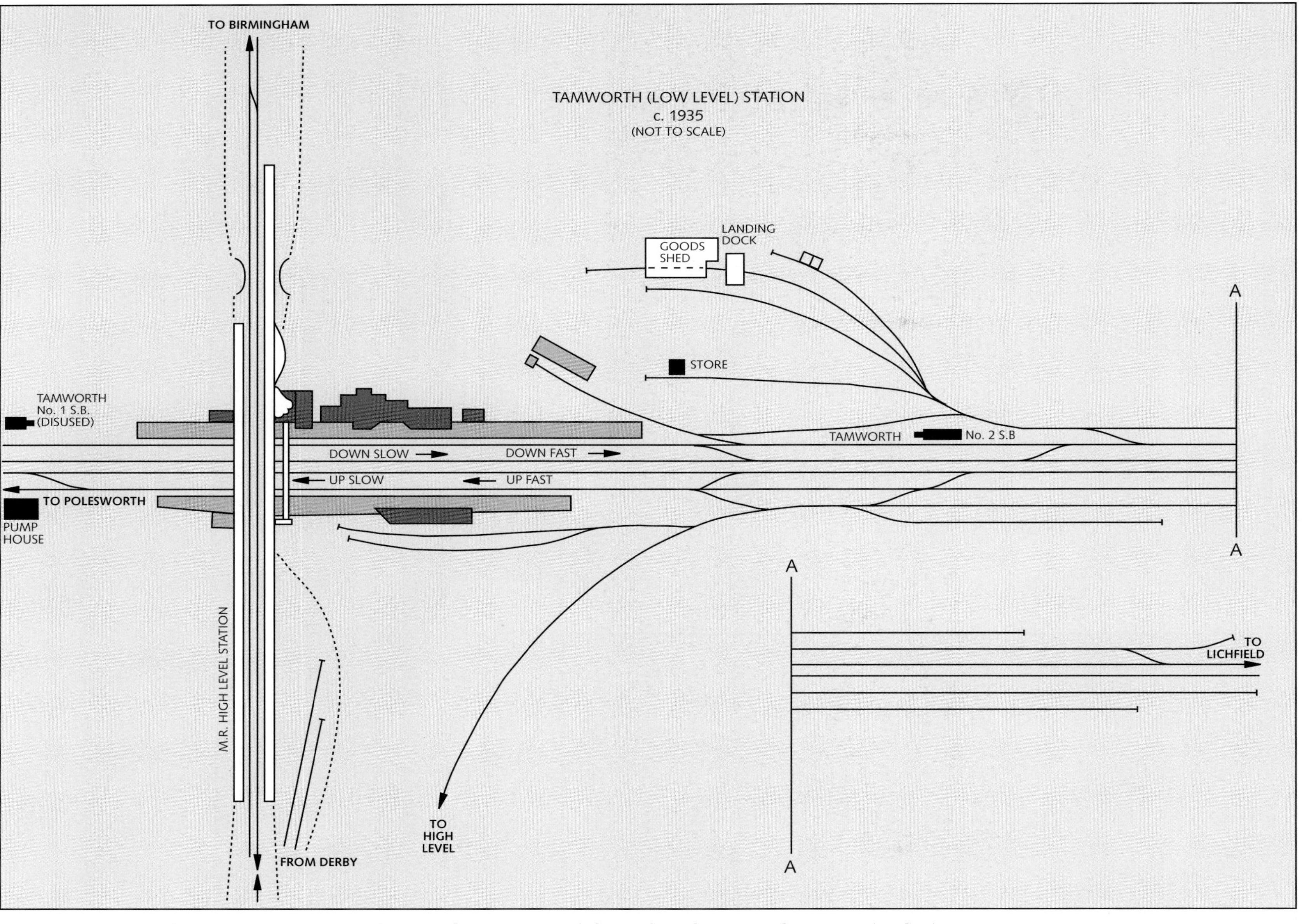

A plan of Tamworth station in the 1930s, showing the proximity of the High and Low Level stations. *(Author)*

Fowler-designed LMS 'Royal Scot' 4–6–0 no. 6163 *Civil Service Rifleman* at the head of the Down 'Irish Mail' passing through Tamworth in 1931. The 'Irish Mail' was involved in an accident here on 4 September 1870. There were two reasons why this accident occurred: lack of signals and interlocking points (only partial at Tamworth) and the fact that the two signal-boxes that controlled the TVR at this point were out of sight of each other because the overbridge carrying the MR Bristol–Derby line bisected the station and blocked the view from both these boxes. The station at this time had two platform roads which were loops off the fast lines and the points which controlled them were worked from the two signal-boxes. The 'Irish Mail' was some 13 minutes late as it approached Tamworth. The distant and outer home signals showed clear as the train approached so the driver left the regulator open. The south box signalman was expecting the 'Mail' and set his road accordingly, which meant that the Up platform road was open to the sidings. The north box signalman was confused because his watch had stopped and he was expecting a goods train, so he had set his road for the Up platform. When he saw the light of the approaching 'Irish Mail' he thought it was a light engine. The 'Mail' ran over the crossover and through the Up platform road, along the dead-end siding, then went through the stop block at the end of the siding, landing upright in the river. One passenger and the driver were killed, and the guard was seriously injured. The accident could have been avoided if the south box signalman had realised his error and reset his points so that the train could regain the Up fast line. The inspector blamed a lack of communication for the accident, as well as obvious defects in signalling and points control. *(Author's Collection)*

An unidentified LMS 'Black 5' 4–6–0 leaving Tamworth with an Up train on 11 June 1935. Only a few years after the opening of the TVR, the line was honoured by a royal visit when, in 1853, Queen Victoria and Prince Albert traversed the route on their way from Osborne on the Isle of Wight to Balmoral, calling at Tamworth for lunch. The visit to Tamworth was, however, curtailed in an effort to make up time after a delayed sea crossing from the Isle of Wight. Operation of the royal train along the TVR was a rare event, as the royal family usually travelled along the GWR route from Paddington to Wolverhampton, gaining LNWR metals at Bushbury for the remainder of the journey to Scotland. *(R. Carpenter)*

Ex-LMS rebuilt 'Patriot' Class 4–6–0 no. 45523 *Bangor* passes under the MR line as it heads out of Tamworth with an Up express. *(R. Carpenter)*

Ex-LMS 'Princess-Coronation' Pacific no. 46256 *Sir William A. Stanier FRS* passing Tamworth with a Down express in 1956. *(R. Carpenter)*

Ex-LMS 'Princess-Coronation' Pacific no. 46240 *City of Coventry* hauls an Up express through Tamworth in the late 1950s. *(R. Carpenter)*

Ex-LMS 2P 4–4–0 no. 40652 leaves Tamworth at the head of a local train for Stafford in the mid-1950s. MR-designed or influenced engines appeared on the TVR following the Grouping of 1923, when locomotive design was concentrated at Derby, and considerable MR influence was exerted for the first decade. Such small engines, which were used on top-link trains at that time, proved incapable of coping with heavy traffic and this led to trials with GWR 'Castle' Class 4–6–0 no. 5000 *Launceston Castle* on Scottish expresses, and this became a familiar sight on the TVR. Such was its success that the LMS asked the GWR to build some for them. The GWR refused, but the trials led to the construction of the famous 'Royal-Scot' Class 4–6–0s and to the LMS bringing William Stanier from Swindon to Crewe. His LMS express designs, the 'Princess-Royal' and 'Princess-Coronation' Pacifics, dominated expresses along the TVR until the end of steam traction. *(R. Carpenter)*

An express approaches Tamworth double-headed by 'Patriot' Class 4–6–0 no. 45510 and rebuilt 'Royal-Scot' 4–6–0 *Royal Scot* itself at the end of the 1950s. Vandalism is often regarded as a new phenomenon, but this is not altogether true. In the first year of BR ownership the railways suffered widely from this problem and trainspotters were banned at many stations. One of the first stations to impose such a ban was Tamworth, after track and installations had been damaged. *(R. Carpenter)*

Ex-War Department 2–8–0, as BR no. 90512, being re-railed at Tamworth following an accident on 28 April 1951. *(H.C. Casserley)*

The High Level station in Tamworth was rebuilt in 1962. Formerly owned by the Midland Railway, it was the reason why the TVR placed so much importance on Tamworth, and why it was of such value for mail interchange. *(Revd D. Hardy)*

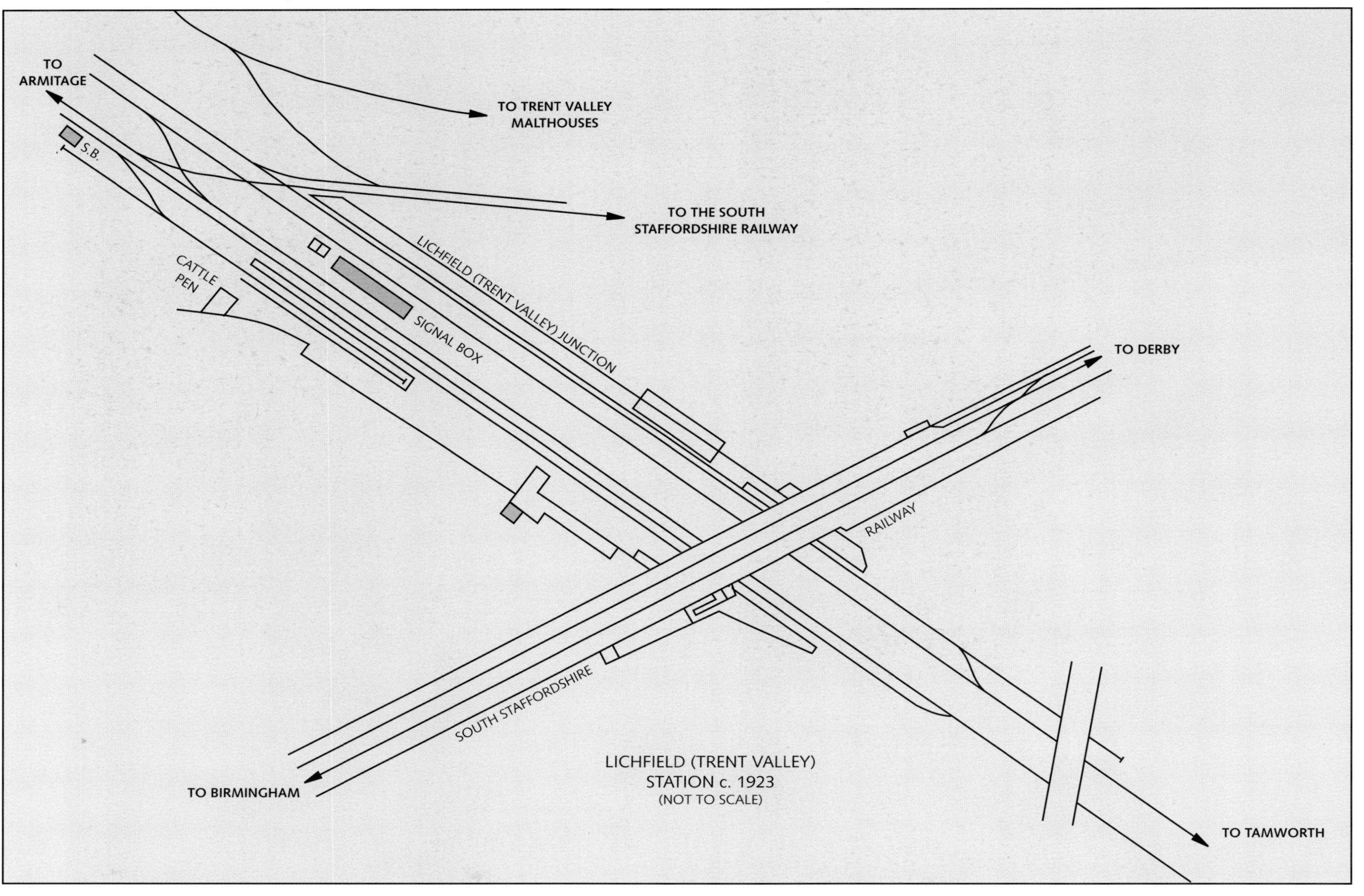

A plan of Lichfield (Trent Valley) station, *c.* 1923. Also shown on the plan is the South Staffordshire Railway line between Birmingham and Derby, which crossed the TVR here, with the SSR Lichfield station also in view. The SSR junction, at top left of the plan, closed to passengers in January 1965, although it remained open to freight for a few years longer. *(Author)*

Ex-LMS rebuilt 'Patriot' Class 4–6–0 no. 45540 *Sir Richard Turnbull* passes through Lichfield (Trent Valley) with the Down 'Comet' express for Manchester (London Road), *c.* 1956. This train left the TVR at Colwich and ran to Manchester over North Staffordshire metals, via Stoke-on-Trent. Lichfield (Trent Valley) station was one of the original TVR stations and the John Livock-designed buildings, in the usual Jacobean style for 'First Class' stations, were substantial. Visible at the far end of the station is the bridge which carried the SSR Birmingham–Derby line over the TVR. Its station, Lichfield City, now Lichfield (Trent Valley) High Level, still has a train service, being the terminus of the 'Cross-City' line from Redditch, Longbridge, Birmingham (New Street) and Sutton Coldfield. *(R. Carpenter)*

Ex-LMS 2P 4–4–0 no. 40692, having propelled the Walsall District Engineer Saloon no. M45044M through Lichfield (Trent Valley) station, hauls it along the spur to the SSR line on 7 May 1959, in order to return to Walsall via Hammerwich and Pelsall. *(F.W. Shuttleworth)*

BR Class 2 2–6–0 no. 78030 resting at Lichfield (Trent Valley) with saloon no. M45010M in the BR carmine and cream livery of that period. This carriage was converted in 1917 from Midland Railway steam railcar no. 2234 for the MR Superintendent of the line. It is seen here as the vehicle of the Signal and Telegraph Engineer, Crewe. *(F.W. Shuttleworth)*

Another Down 'Comet' for Manchester heading through Lichfield (Trent Valley) station, hauled by BR 'Britannia' Pacific no. 70033 *Charles Dickens*, in 1955. The station seen here opened on 3 March 1871, replacing the original, which had been opened on 15 September 1847 and stood a quarter of a mile further north. This new station was built to link with the SSR's station which opened on the same day. *(R. Carpenter)*

Preparing to leave Lichfield (Trent Valley) at the head of a Down express on 20 April 1957 are ex-LMS 2–6–4 tank no. 42489 and an unidentified ex-LMS 'Jubilee' Class 4–6–0. As well as being famed for its three-spired cathedral, Lichfield was the birthplace of Dr Samuel Johnson who created the first English dictionary. The town was also home to David Garrick and Anna Sewell, author of the children's classic *Black Beauty*. *(R. Carpenter)*

A signalman/lampman servicing the lamps and signals at Lichfield (Trent Valley) in the mid-1950s. *(R. Carpenter)*

Table 11

THE WELSHMAN

THROUGH RESTAURANT CAR EXPRESS TRAIN BETWEEN LONDON and NORTH WALES

WEEKDAYS

		Mondays to Fridays		Saturdays only	
		am		am	
London (Euston)	dep	11 15		11 15	
		pm		pm	
Rugby (L.M.R.)	,,	12 54		12 57	
Crewe	,,	2 37		....	
Beeston Castle	,,	2 53		..	
Chester (General)	arr	3 8		3 8	
Chester (General)	dep	3 15	3 23	3 15	3 23
Prestatyn	arr	....	3 55	....	3 56
Rhyl	,,	..	4 2	..	4 4
Abergele	,,	....	4 13	....	4 17
Colwyn Bay	,,	..	4 25	..	4 30
Llandudno Junction	,,	....	4 33	....	4 38
Deganwy	arr	..	4 41	..	4 48
Llandudno	,,	....	4 46	....	4 53
Penmaenmawr	arr	4 12	..	4 12	..
Llanfairfechan	,,	4 20	....	4 20	....
Bangor	,,	4 31	..	4 31	..
Menai Bridge	,,	4 44	....	4 44	....
Port Dinorwic	,,	4 50	..	4 50	..
Caernarvon	,,	4 59	....	4 59	....
Penygroes	,,	5 22	..	5 22	..
Brynkir	,,	5 35	....	5 35	....
Chwilog	,,	5 46	..	5 46	..
Afonwen	,,	5 50	....	5 50	....
Pwllheli	arr	6 10	..	6 10	..
Criccieth	arr	6 3	....	6 3	....
Portmadoc	,,	6 12	..	6 12	..

		Mondays to Fridays		Saturdays only	
			am		am
Portmadoc	dep	..	11 0	..	9 55
Criccieth	,,	....	11 9	....	10 4
Pwllheli	dep	..	11 0	..	10 0
Afonwen	dep	....	11 25	....	10 25
Chwilog	,,	..	11 29	..	10 29
Brynkir	,,	....	11 42	....	10 42
Penygroes	,,	..	11 54	..	10 54
Groeslon	,,	....	11 58	....	10 58
			pm		
Caernarvon	,,	..	12 16	..	11 16
Menai Bridge	,,	....	12 28	....	11 28
Bangor	,,	.	12 45	..	11 45
Llanfairfechan	,,	....	12 56	....	11 57
					pm
Penmaenmawr	,,	pm	1 3	pm	12 5
Llandudno	dep	1 0	....	12 14	....
Deganwy	,,	1 5	..	..	..
Llandudno Junction	dep	1 24		12 34	
Colwyn Bay	,,	1 32		12 45	
Rhyl	,,	1 51		1 7	
Prestatyn	,,	1 59		..	
Chester (General)	,,	2 40		1 53	
Beeston Castle	,,	2 58		..	
Crewe	arr	3 15		....	
Stafford	,,	3 56		..	
London (Euston)	,,	6 28		5 34	

Through Carriages between London and Llandudno, Pwllheli, Portmadoc.
Restaurant Car between London and Bangor.

A timetable for 'The Welshman' express which ran from Euston to resorts in North Wales, traversing the TVR. *(Author's Collection)*

Armitage station, *c* 1900. A local LNWR train is just departing. The station opened on 15 September 1847 as a secondary stopping place. Although the buildings are entirely of timber, it was created by John Livock, who designed all of the splendid Jacobean-style structures associated with the TVR 'First Class' stations. The original Nuneaton station may have looked like this, given that when it opened it too was only a secondary stopping place. Armitage station served a sanitary pottery works nearby. Armitage Ware (nowadays known as Armitage-Shanks) became famous worldwide for its toilets, baths and washbasins and still produces such goods at the same location today. The pottery works here led to the construction of a goods station at Armitage, which opened on 1 October 1877. Armitage station was officially closed on 13 June 1960, as the TVR was being prepared for electrification. However, the last trains to call at Armitage were on Saturday 11 June, the station not then being served by Sunday trains. *(Author's Collection)*

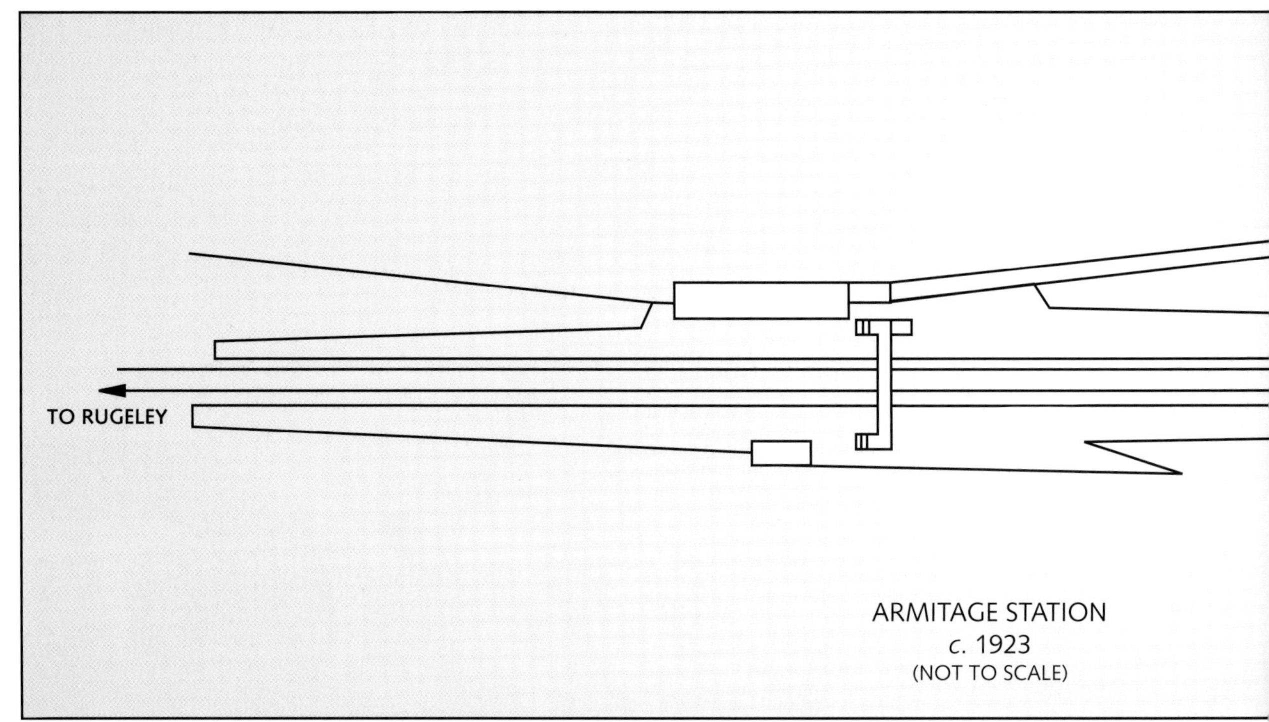

A dirty-looking streamlined ex-LMS 'Princess-Coronation' Pacific at the head of an express just south of Rugeley in early BR days. *(F.W. Shuttleworth)*

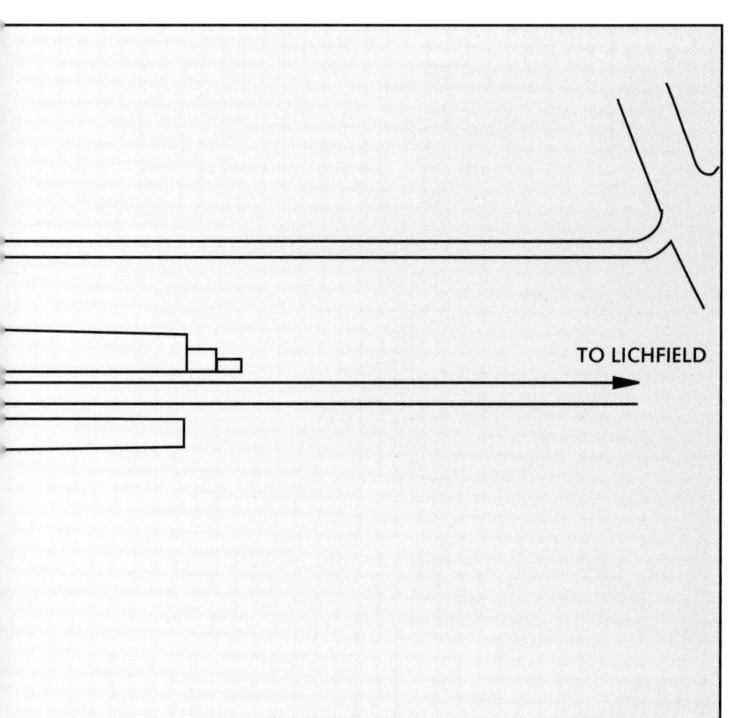

The simple layout at Armitage station, *c.* 1923. *(Author)*

An Up express, hauled by an unidentified LMS 'Royal Scot' Class 4–6–0, passes by a signal gantry controlling the Down lines just south of Rugeley in the late 1930s. Just visible on the left is the branch to Hednesford, which opened on 1 August 1850. *(F.W. Shuttleworth)*

A plan of the important station at Rugeley *c.* 1923. *(Author)*

A general view of Rugeley station, another of the 'First Class' stations, *c.* 1900. Until the SSR line to Cannock closed in 1965, Rugeley was a junction, the SSR serving the coalfields of South Staffordshire and providing much coal traffic along the TVR. In the 1850s the residents of Rugeley wanted to change the name of the town and sent a deputation to the Prime Minister, Lord Palmerston, for permission to do so. The prime minister was not in favour of a change but cheekily suggested that the town be called 'Palmerston' after himself. However, this recalled the town's unfortunate associations with one Dr Palmer, who poisoned his wealthy patients with strychnine. Thereafter the idea of a name change was quietly forgotten. *(Author's Collection)*

WALSALL, CANNOCK, AND RUGELEY. 51

For local trains pages	WEEK DAYS	a.m.	a.m.		a.m.	noon		p.m.	p.m.	p.m.		p.m.		p.m.	SUNDAYS a.m.	SUNDAYS p.m.
48	Birmingham (New Street) dep	6 10	7 40	...	9 25	12 15		2 20	4 25	5 25		7 22		*8 45*	9 10	5 10
	Dudley ,,	.	7 50	.	9 35	12 15		2 35	4 40	5 30		7 10		*9 0*	9 30	5 25
61	Wolverhampton (H. Level) ,,	6 25	7 50	...	9 30	12 30		2 25	4 40	5 35		7 20		*9 7*	9 15	5 15
	WALSALL	**6 48**	**8 20**	.	**10 5**	**1 2**		**3 0**	**5 10**	**6 5**		**7 58**		**9 30**	**10 5**	**5 48**
	Birchills	...	8 24	...	10 9	1 7		3 4	5 15	...		8 2		...	...	...
	Bloxwich	6 55	8 28	.	10 13	1 12		3 8	5 19	6 12		8 6		*9 37*	10 14	5 55
	Wyrley and Church Bridge	7 3	8 36	...	10 18	1 21		3 13	5 27	6 21		8 13		*9 44*	10 22	6 3
	Cannock	7 8	8 40	.	10 23	1 27		3 18	5 32	6 26		8 18		*9 49*	10 27	6 8
	Hednesford	7 15	8 46	...	10 30	1 34		3 25	5 39	6 33		8 25		*9 57*	10 34	6 15
	RUGELEY Town arr	**7 26**	**8 56**	.	**10 41**	**1 45**		**3 36**	**5 50**	**6 44**		**8 35**		.	**10 45**	**6 26**
	RUGELEY Trent Valley ,,	7 29	8 59	...	10 44	1 50		3 39	5 54	6 47		8 38		...	10 48	6 29
43	Rugeley (Trent Valley) ...dep	8 44	9 34	.	10 47	2 20		3 50	6 30	.		.		Tuesdays and Saturdays only.	12 58	.
	Rugby arr	10 5	10 43	...	12 15	4 17		5 25	8 7	...		...			2 15	...
42	**RUGELEY** (Trent Valley) dep	7 33	9 27	.	11 0	1 55	2 10	3 52	5 59	7 2	7 7	8 49	8 50		10 51	6 30
	Colwich	7 40	9 34	...	11 6	2 1	2 15	3 59	6 7	...	7 12	...	8 57		11 0	6 36
	Stoke (N. S. Rly.) arr	9 10	.	.	11 54	2 55	.	.	.	.	8†0	.	.		.	8 8
	Macclesfield (N. S. Rly.) ,,	10 42	...	...	2 42	3 47	...	...	...	...	...	...	...		...	9 30
	Manchester (via Stoke) ... ,,	11 19	.	.	3 29	4 20	.	.	.	.	.	.	.		.	10 36
42	Milford and Brocton ,,	7 45	9 39	...	11 12	...	2 21	4 5	6 12	...	...	...	9 2		11 5	6 41
	STAFFORD ,,	**7 55**	**9 48**		**11 20**	.	**2 29**	**4 13**	**6 22**	**7 17**	.	**9 5**	**9 12**	.	**11 15**	**6 50**

	WEEK DAYS.	a.m.	a.m.	a.m.	Th a.m.	noon	p.m.	noon	p.m.	p.m.		p.m.		SUNDAYS a.m.	SUNDAYS p.m.
46	**STAFFORD** dep	**6 50**	**8 10**	**9 21**	*10 30*	**12 9**	**2 0**	...	**3 45**	**6 10**	...	**8 40**	...	**8 30**	**8 0**
	Milford and Brocton ,,	6 58	8 18	.	*10 37*	12 8	2 8	.	3 53	6 18	.	8 48	.	8 38	8 8
	Manchester (via Stoke) ... ,,	...	...	...	...	8 30	...	12 0	...	3 20	...	...	...	...	11 15
	Macclesfield (N. S. Rly.) ,,	.	.	.	.	9 15	.	12 35	.	4 8	.	.	.	.	12 55
	Stoke (N. S. Rly.) ,,	...	7 20	...	...	10 15	...	2 25	...	6 5	...	...	...	...	2 30
45	Colwich ,,	7 5	8 22	.	*10 41*	12 12	2 12	§	3 58	6 50	.	8 52	.	8 42	8 12
	RUGELEY (Trent Valley) arr	7 13	8 29	9 34	*10 47*	12 20	2 20	...	4 4	6 56	...	8 58	...	8 48	8 18
61	Rugby dep	.	7 12	7 15	*10 0*	10 0	11 5	.	2 25	6 2	.	7 28	.	.	.
	Rugeley (Trent Valley) ... arr	...	8 14	9 27	*11 34*	11 34	2 10	...	3 52	6 58	...	8 49	...	...	...
	RUGELEY Tre't Valley dep	7 15	8 35	9 48	*11 57*	12 25	2 45	.	4 30	7 5	.	9 0	.	8 52	8 23
	RUGELEY Town ,,	**7 18**	**8 38**	**9 51**	**12 0**	**12 29**	**2 49**	...	**4 34**	**7 8**	...	**9 3**	...	**8 55**	**8 26**
	Hednesford	7 30	8 50	10 3	*12 10*	12 42	3 2	.	4 48	7 20	.	9 16	.	9 8	8 39
	Cannock	7 35	8 55	10 8	*12 15*	12 47	3 7	...	4 54	7 25	...	9 21	...	9 13	8 44
	Wyrley and Church Bridge	7 39	8 59	10 12	*12 19*	12 51	3 11	.	4 58	7 29	.	9 25	.	9 17	8 48
	Bloxwich	7 48	9 8	10 21	...	1 0	3 20	...	5 7	7 38	...	9 34	...	9 26	8 57
	Birchills	7 53	.	10 26	.	1 5	3 25	.	5 13	7 43	.	.	.	.	.
	WALSALL arr	**7 58**	**9 15**	**10 30**	**12 34**	**1 10**	**3 30**	...	**5 18**	**7 47**	...	**9 40**	...	**9 35**	**9 5**
61	Wolverhampton (H. Level) arr	8 42	9 55	11 6	*12 56*	1 54	3 55	.	5 48	8 43	.	10 28	.	11 20	10 20
	Dudley ,,	8 55	10 2	11 0	...	1 43	4 55	...	5 48	8 8	...	10 42	...	10 22	10 10
66	Birmingham (New Street) ,,	8 35	10 13	10 57	*1 5*	2 0	4 10	.	6 0	8 25	.	11 5	.	10 28	10 15

†—Arrives at Stoke at 8.47 p.m. on Mondays, Thursdays, and Saturdays.

§—Arrives at Colwich at 3.18 p.m.

Th—Thursdays only.

A timetable for SSR train services between Walsall and Rugeley in LNWR days. These trains connected with TVR expresses at Rugeley (Trent Valley). *(Author's Collection)*

Passing Rugeley no. 2 signal-box is ex-LMS 'Crab' 2–6–0 no. 42920 with an Up fitted freight train in 1959. The passenger footbridge at Rugeley station can be seen here, along with the busy goods yard which closed to freight traffic in May 1964. *(R. Carpenter)*

BR 'Britannia' Pacific no. 70031 *Byron* passes through Rugeley (Trent Valley) station in 1956 at the head of the Down 'Mancunian'. 'Trent Valley' was added to the station name in 1917. *(R. Carpenter)*

The SSR station at Rugeley opened on 1 June 1870 and was the source of hopeless confusion between the station names in the town. The SSR station was known as Rugeley (Trent Valley) in branch timetables, while the TVR station was known simply as Rugeley. This confusion was finally resolved during the First World War, when it was laid down that Rugeley (Trent Valley) was the only name for the station on the TVR route, this ruling being effective from 15 April 1917. The SSR station, by then under LNWR control, was retitled Rugeley Town. *(Author's Collection)*

Table 71

RUGELEY, CANNOCK AND WALSALL

WEEKDAYS

Miles	Station	SO a.m.	SX a.m.	a.m.	a.m.	SX a.m.	a.m.	TC—Stafford to Birmingham	a.m. (TC—Rugeley (T.V.) to Birmingham)		a.m.	
—	50 Stoke-on-Trent	...	...	...	...	...	6 48			...	8 43	...
0	**Stafford** dep.	.	.	5 40	.	.	8 0			.	9 54	.
4	Milford and Brocton (Closed)	...	...	...	...	...	...			...	...	...
6½	Colwich	.	.	.	.	.	8 12			.	.	.
9¼	**Rugeley** (T.V.) arr.	...	...	5 57	...	...	8 18			...	10 5	...
—	Rugby dep.	.	.	.	.	.	.		7 30	.	9 4	.
—	Rugeley (T.V.) arr.	...	...	...	...	...	...		9 11	...	10 15	...
—	**Rugeley** T.V. dep.	5 35	5 41	6 5	7 21	.	8 22		9 36	.	11 0	.
10¼	**Rugeley** Town	5 39	5 46	6 8	7 26	...	8 26		9 39	...	11 3	...
12½	Brindley Heath	5 46	5 54	6 15	7 33	.	8 33		9 46	.	11 10	.
14¾	Hednesford	5 55	6 5	6 24	7 41	8 18	8 41		9 54	...	11 18	...
16½	Cannock	6 06	6D16	6 31	7 49	8 24	8 48		10 1	.	11 25	.
18	Wyrley and Cheslyn Hay	6 10	6 20	6 35	7 53	8 28	8 52		10 5	...	11 29	...
21½	Bloxwich	6 20	6 30	6 44	8 2	8 37	9 1		10 14	.	11 38	.
24½	**Walsall** arr.	6 28	6 38	6 52	8 10	8 45	9 9		10 22	...	11 46	...
31¼	68 Wolverhampton (H.L.) arr.	...	...	7 17	8 40	...	9 30		...	...	12C21	...
31	74 Dudley „	.	.	7 45	8 44	.	.		.	.	12S020	.
35½	68 Birmingham (New St.) „	...	7 31	7B44	8 52	...	9 52		10 47	...	12 27	...

Miles	Station	p.m.	SO p.m.	p.m.	TC—Stafford to Birmingham	SO p.m.	p.m.	p.m.		SX p.m.	SO p.m.		p.m.	
—	50 Stoke-on-Trent	10R55	...	12 39		...	...	3 40	...	...	5 17	...	6 47	...
0	**Stafford** dep.	12S010	.	2 2		.	.	4 32	.	.	6 10	.	8 22	.
4	Milford and Brocton (Closed)	...	...	...		...	...	...	...	..	...	...	.	...
6½	Colwich	.	.	2 13		.	.	4 42	.	.	6 20	.	8 33	.
9¼	**Rugeley** (T.V.) arr.	12S022	...	2 19		...	...	4 48	...	...	6 26	...	8 39	...
—	Rugby dep.	10†30	.	12G40		1 57	.	.	.	.	5 22	.	.	.
—	Rugeley (T.V.) arr.	11F53	...	1 57		3 5	...	...	...	...	6 30	...	...	...
—	**Rugeley** T.V. dep.	12 43	1 39	2 25		3 20	4 23	5 20	.	.	6 34	.	8 47	.
10¼	**Rugeley** Town	12 46	1 42	2 28		3 23	4D30	5 23	...	6 24	6 37	...	8 50	...
12½	Brindley Heath	12 53	1 49	2 35		3 30	4 38	5 30	.	6 31	6 44	.	8 57	.
14¾	Hednesford	1 1	1 57	2 43		3 38	4 46	5 38	...	6 40	6 52	...	9 5	...
16½	Cannock	1 8	2 4	2 50		3D49	4 53	5 45	.	6 48	6 59	.	9 12	.
18	Wyrley and Cheslyn Hay	1 12	2 8	2 54		3 53	4 57	5 49	...	6 52	7 3	...	9 16	...
21½	Bloxwich	1 21	2 17	3 3		4 2	5 6	5 58	.	7 2	7 12	.	9 25	.
24½	**Walsall** arr.	1 29	2 25	3 11		4 11	5 14	6 6	...	7 10	7 20	...	9 33	...
31¼	68 Wolverhampton (H.L.) arr.	2 0	...	...		...	5 39	7H 6	...	8 30	7 50	...	10 20	...
31	74 Dudley „	2 4	.	.		.	5SX49	7 8	.	8 19	.	.	10S03	.
35½	68 Birmingham (New St.) „	2 13	3 4	3 51		4 52	6 25	7SX17	...	7 56	7 56	...	10 11	...

SUNDAYS

Station	a.m.		p.m.		p.m.		p.m.	p.m.		p.m.	p.m.			
50 Stoke-on-Trent	...	...	...	...	10† 0	..	...	...	...	6 20	7 55	...	...	...
Stafford dep.	.	.	.	.	1 31	.	.	.	.	7 40	9 20	.	.	.
Milford and Brocton (Closed)	...	...	...	...	...	...	...	...	...	...	...	...	...	...
Colwich	.	.	.	.	.	.	.	.	.	.	.	.	.	.
Rugeley (T.V.) arr.	...	...	...	...	1 49	...	...	...	...	7 54	9 33	...	...	...
Rugby dep.	.	.	10†50	.	.	.	.	.	.	.	7 33	.	.	.
Rugeley (T.V.) arr.	...	...	12 17	...	...	...	...	...	...	...	9 7	...	...	...
Rugeley T.V. dep.	8 10	.	12 35	.	2 20	.	4 35	6 25	.	8 30	9 37	.	.	.
Rugeley Town	8 13	...	12 38	...	2 23	...	4 38	6 28	...	8 33	9 43	...	...	...
Brindley Heath	8 20	.	12 45	.	2 30	.	4 45	6 36	.	8 40	9 50	.	.	.
Hednesford	8 28	...	12 53	...	2 38	...	4 53	6 45	...	8 48	9 58	...	...	...
Cannock	8 35	.	1 0	.	2 45	.	5 0	6 53	.	8 55	10 5	.	.	.
Wyrley and Cheslyn Hay	8 39	...	1 4	...	2 49	...	5 4	6 58	...	8 59	10 9	...	...	...
Bloxwich	8 48	.	1 13	.	2 58	.	5 13	7 8	.	9 8	10 18	.	.	.
Walsall arr.	8 56	...	1 21	...	3 6	...	5 21	7 16	...	9 16	10 26	...	...	...
68 Wolverhampton (H.L.) arr.	9 20	...	...	...	...	...	5 42	...	...	10 6	...	...	...	...
74 Dudley „	.	.	.	.	.	.	.	.	.	.	.	.	.	.
68 Birmingham (New St.) „	9 36	...	2 0	...	3 41	...	...	8 1	...	10 3	...	...	...	...

WEEKDAYS

Miles	Station	a.m.	a.m.	TC—Birmingham to Stafford	SX a.m.	a.m.	a.m.	a.m.	p.m.	p.m.	p.m.	p.m.	p.m.
—	68 Birmingham (New St.) dep.	...	5 55		6 33	7 37	8 35	9 45	12 15	1 20	2A35	4 12	5 26
—	74 Dudley „	.	.		7 20	.	8 40	.	12S033	1 12	.	.	5 5
—	68 Wolverhampton (H.L.) „	...	...		7 15	7 15	8 27	9 19	10 57	1N10	2K34	...	5 22
0	**Walsall** dep.	6 10	6 40		7 45	8 16	9 10	10 31	12 56	1 59	3 25	5 18	5 55
3	Bloxwich	6 18	6 48		7 53	8 24	9 18	10 39	1 6	2 7	3 33	5 26	6 3
6½	Wyrley and Cheslyn Hay	6 25	6 55		8 0	8 31	9 25	10 46	1 13	2 14	3 40	5 33	6 10
8	Cannock	6 30	7 1		8 5	8 36	9 30	10 51	1 18	2 19	3 45	5 38	6 15
9¾	Hednesford	6 37	7 9		8 12	8 43	9 37	10 58	1 25	2 26	3 52	5 45	6 22
12	Brindley Heath	6 42	7 14		...	8 48	9 42	11 3	1 30	2 31	3 57	5 50	6 27
14¼	**Rugeley** Town arr.	6 47	7 20		.	8 54	9 48	11 9	1 35	2 36	4 2	5 55	6 33
15¼	**Rugeley** T.V. „	6 51	7 24		...	8 58	9 52	11 13	1 39	2 40	4 6	5 59	6 37
—	Rugeley (T.V.) dep.	.	7 55		.	.	10 6	.	2B 0	.	4 57	6 28	.
57	Rugby arr.	...	9 39		...	...	11 24	...	3B19	...	6 43	7 57	...
—	**Rugeley** (T.V.) dep.	.	7 25		.	9 11	10 15	11 25	1M54	2P58	.	6 30	.
18	Colwich	...	7 30		...	9 17	...	11 30	2M 0	...	...	6 35	...
20½	Milford and Brocton (Closed) dep.	.	.		.	...	...	...	.	.	.	.	.
24½	**Stafford** arr.	...	7 41		...	9 28	10 29	11 40	2M11	3P11	...	6 46	...
40½	Stoke-on-Trent arr.	.	8 28		.	10E10	11 31	1 21	.	4 26	.	7 58	.

Miles	Station		p.m.	SX p.m.	p.m.		p.m.	SO p.m.	SX p.m.		SO p.m.	
—	68 Birmingham (New St.) dep.	...	6 7	6 33	7 12	...	8 36	9 25	10 35	...	10 47	...
—	74 Dudley „	.	5SX54	.	7 15	.	.	.	10 30	.	10 30	.
—	68 Wolverhampton (H.L.) „	...	5L57	6 40	6 40	...	8S036	...	10 35	...	10 35	...
0	**Walsall** dep.	.	6 45	7 22	7 55	.	9 20	10 0	11 16	.	11 25	.
3	Bloxwich	...	6 55	7 30	8 3	...	9 28	10 8	11 24	...	11 33	...
6½	Wyrley and Cheslyn Hay	.	7 2	7 37	8 10	.	9 35	10 15	11 33	.	11 42	.
8	Cannock	...	7 7	7 42	8 15	...	9 40	10 20	11 39	...	11 49	...
9¾	Hednesford	.	7 14	7 49	8 22	.	9 48	10 27	11 49	.	12 1	.
12	Brindley Heath	...	7 20	...	8 28	...	9 53	10 33	11 56	...	12 8	...
14¼	**Rugeley** Town arr.	.	7 26	7 58	8 34	.	9 58	10 39	12 1	.	12 14	.
15¼	**Rugeley** T.V. „	...	7 30	8 2	8 38	...	10 2	10 43	12 5	...	12 18	...
—	Rugeley (T.V.) dep.	.	.	.	.	.	.	.	.	.	.	.
57	Rugby arr.	...	...	...	...	...	...	...	...	...	...	...
—	**Rugeley** (T.V.) dep.	.	.	.	9 4	.	.	.	.	.	.	.
18	Colwich	...	...	...	...	...	...	...	...	...	...	...
20½	Milford and Brocton (Closed) dep.	.	.	.	...	.	.	.	.	.	.	.
24½	**Stafford** arr.	...	...	...	9 18	...	...	...	...	...	...	...
40½	Stoke-on-Trent arr.	.	.	.	10 10	.	.	.	.	.	.	.

SUNDAYS

Station	a.m.	a.m.	a.m.		p.m.	p.m.	p.m.	p.m.	p.m.	p.m.				
68 Birmingham (New St.) dep.	...	9 25	...	...	12 45	2 30	4 33	5 50	9 40	10 45	...	...	...	...
74 Dudley „	.	.	.	.	.	.	.	.	.	.	.	.	.	.
68 Wolverhampton (H.L.) „	...	9 30	11 7	...	...	1 28	...	...	..	10 15	...	...	...	...
Walsall dep.	6 40	10 15	11 29	.	1 24	3 30	5 15	6 50	10 17	11 20	.	.	.	.
Bloxwich	6 48	10 23	11 37	...	1 32	3 38	5 23	6 38	10 25	11 28	...	...	...	...
Wyrley and Cheslyn Hay	6 55	10 30	11 44	.	1 39	3 45	5 31	6 45	10 32	11 35	.	.	.	.
Cannock	7 1	10 35	11 49	...	1 44	3 50	5 36	6 50	10 37	11 40	...	...	...	...
Hednesford	7 9	10 42	11 56	.	1 51	3 57	5 43	6 57	10 51	11J53	.	.	.	.
Brindley Heath	7 14	10 48	12 1	...	1 57	4 2	..	7 2	10 56	11 58	...	...	...	...
Rugeley Town arr.	7 20	10 53	12 6	.	2 2	4 7	5 52	7 7	11 1	12 4	.	.	.	.
Rugeley T.V. „	7 24	10 57	12 10	...	2 6	4 11	5 56	7 11	11 5	12 8	...	...	...	...
Rugeley (T.V.) dep.	.	.	1 51	.	.	.	.	8 4	.	.	.	.	.	.
Rugby arr.	...	...	3 26	...	...	...	...	9 22	...	...	...	...	...	...
Rugeley (T.V.) dep.	.	.	12 17	.	.	.	.	9 7	.	.	.	.	.	.
Colwich	...	...	...	...	..	...	...	...	...	...	...	...	...	...
Milford and Brocton (Closed) dep.	.	.	...	.	.	.	.	.	.	.	.	.	.	.
Stafford arr.	...	...	12 32	...	...	...	...	9 21	...	...	...	...	...	...
Stoke-on-Trent arr.	.	.	3 7	.	.	.	.	10 4	.	.	.	.	.	.

†—a.m.
A—On Saturdays departs Birmingham 2.40 p.m.
B—On Saturdays depart Rugeley (T.V.) 2.5 p.m. and arrives Rugby 3.24 p.m.
C—On Sats. arr. Wolverhampton 12.30 p.m.
D—Arrives 4 minutes earlier.
E—On Saturdays arrives Stoke 10.19 a.m.
F—On Sats. arr. Rugeley (T.V.) 12.18 p.m.
G—On Saturdays depart Rugby 12.45 p.m.
H—On Sats. arr. Wolverhampton 6.26 p.m.
J—Arrives 6 minutes earlier.
K—Applies July 29th to September 9th inclusive.
L—Dep. Wolverhampton 6.10 p.m. on Sats.
M—On Saturdays depart Rugeley (T.V.) 1.57 Colwich 2.3, Stafford arrive 2.14 p.m.
N—On Sats. depart Wolverhampton 1.20 p.m.
P—On Saturdays depart Rugeley (T.V.) 3.5, Stafford arrive 3.18 p.m.
R—a.m. and is Saturdays only.
S—On Saturdays arrive Birmingham 7.50 p.m., change at Vauxhall.
SO—Sats. only.
SX—Sats. excepted.
TC—Through Carriage

A BR timetable for trains operating over the SSR line between Walsall and Rugeley. This line closed in January 1965. *(Author's Collection)*

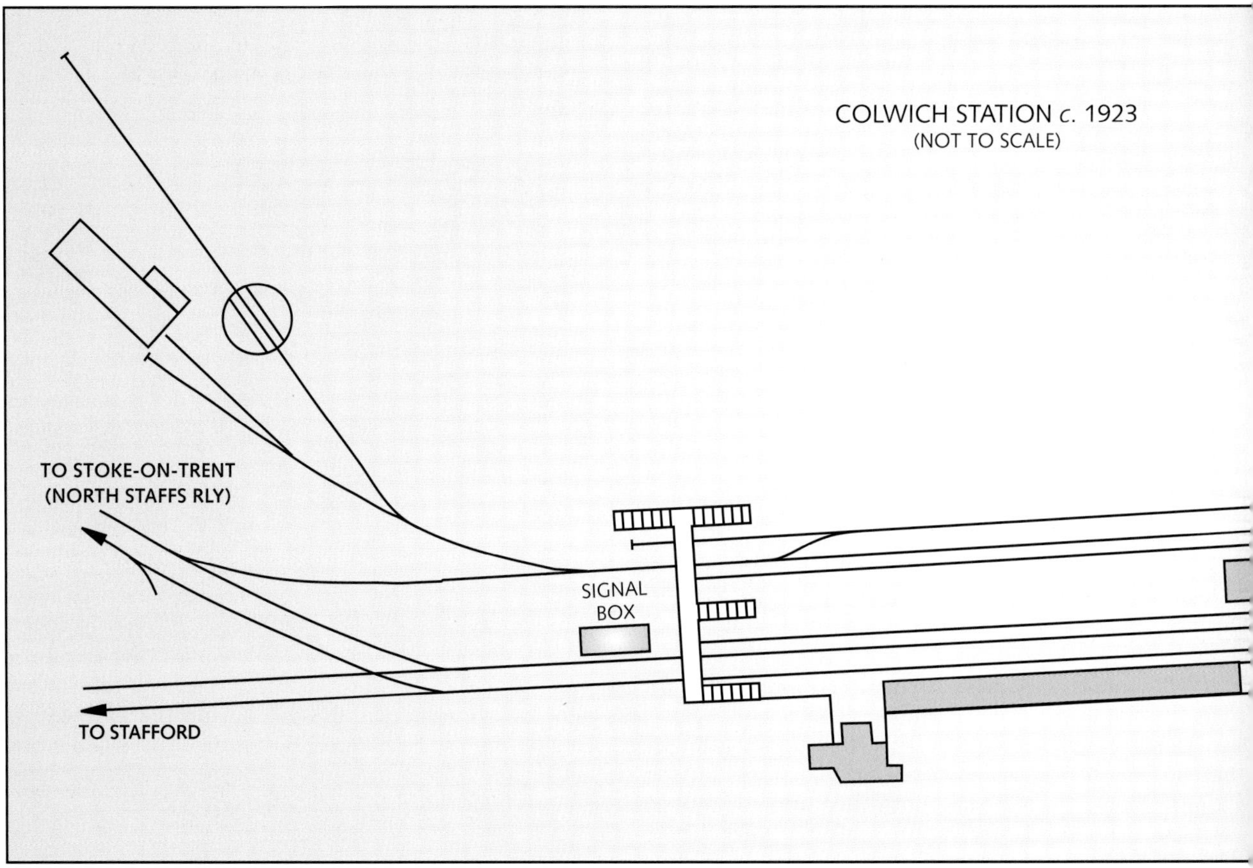

COLWICH STATION *c.* 1923
(NOT TO SCALE)

TO STOKE-ON-TRENT
(NORTH STAFFS RLY)

SIGNAL
BOX

TO STAFFORD

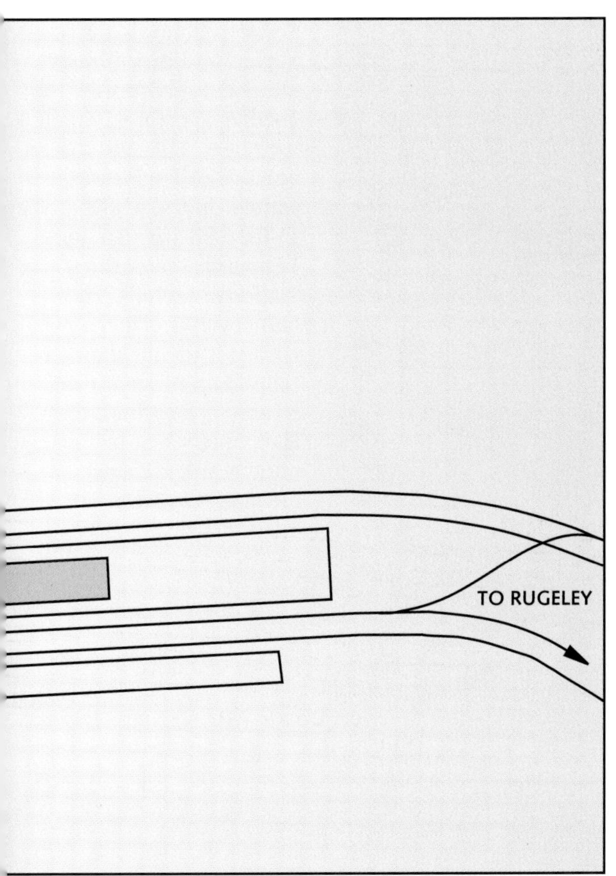

A plan of Colwich station as it appeared in 1923. This was in fact a replacement station built by the LNWR to coincide with the widening to four tracks of the TVR in 1871. *(Author)*

Below: A timetable for 'The Comet' showing its preferred route via Stoke-on-Trent rather than Stafford. *(Author's Collection)*

THE COMET

LONDON (Euston) and MANCHESTER (London Road)

	Mons. to Fris.	Sats. only
	am	am
London (Euston) .... dep	9 45	9 35
	pm	pm
Stoke-on-Trent .. arr	12 34	—
Macclesfield .... ,,	1 8	—
Stockport (Edgeley).. ,,	1 28	1 2
Manchester (Lon. Rd.) ,,	1 41	1 18

	Week-days
	pm
Manchester (London Road) .... dep	5·50
Stockport (Edgeley) .. .. .. ,,	6 4
Crewe .... ,,	6 39
London (Euston) .. .. .. arr	9 36

Restaurant Car Train

Opposite: Colwich station, *c*. 1900. This was one of the original TVR stations when the line opened. The twin pavilioned building seen here replaced the original Jacobean main station building, which was retained as the stationmaster's house when the station was rebuilt in 1871. Colwich was the most northerly of five junctions on the TVR and the station was shared with the North Staffordshire Railway, whose line from Stone was opened on 1 May 1849 and joined the TVR beside the Trent & Mersey Canal. This line was also important to the LNWR which, thanks to the NSR Act of 13 August 1849, had running powers over the Stoke company's metals to Manchester. Although Harecastle Tunnel provided a shorter route it limited the size of motive power and the line was not fully exploited until electrification in the 1960s. The LNWR, LMS, and BR operated Euston–Manchester expresses over the line, thereby avoiding Stafford. The most famous of these trains was 'The Comet'. *(Author's Collection)*

Between Colwich and Milford and Brocton lies Shugborough Tunnel, the northern portal of which is seen here. This was the only major engineering feature on the whole of the TVR and it runs for some 774 yards under the Staffordshire hills. The flamboyant northern portal earned it the nickname of 'The Gates of Jerusalem'. Nearby is Shugborough Hall, family seat of royal photographer Patrick Lichfield. *(D. Ibbotson)*

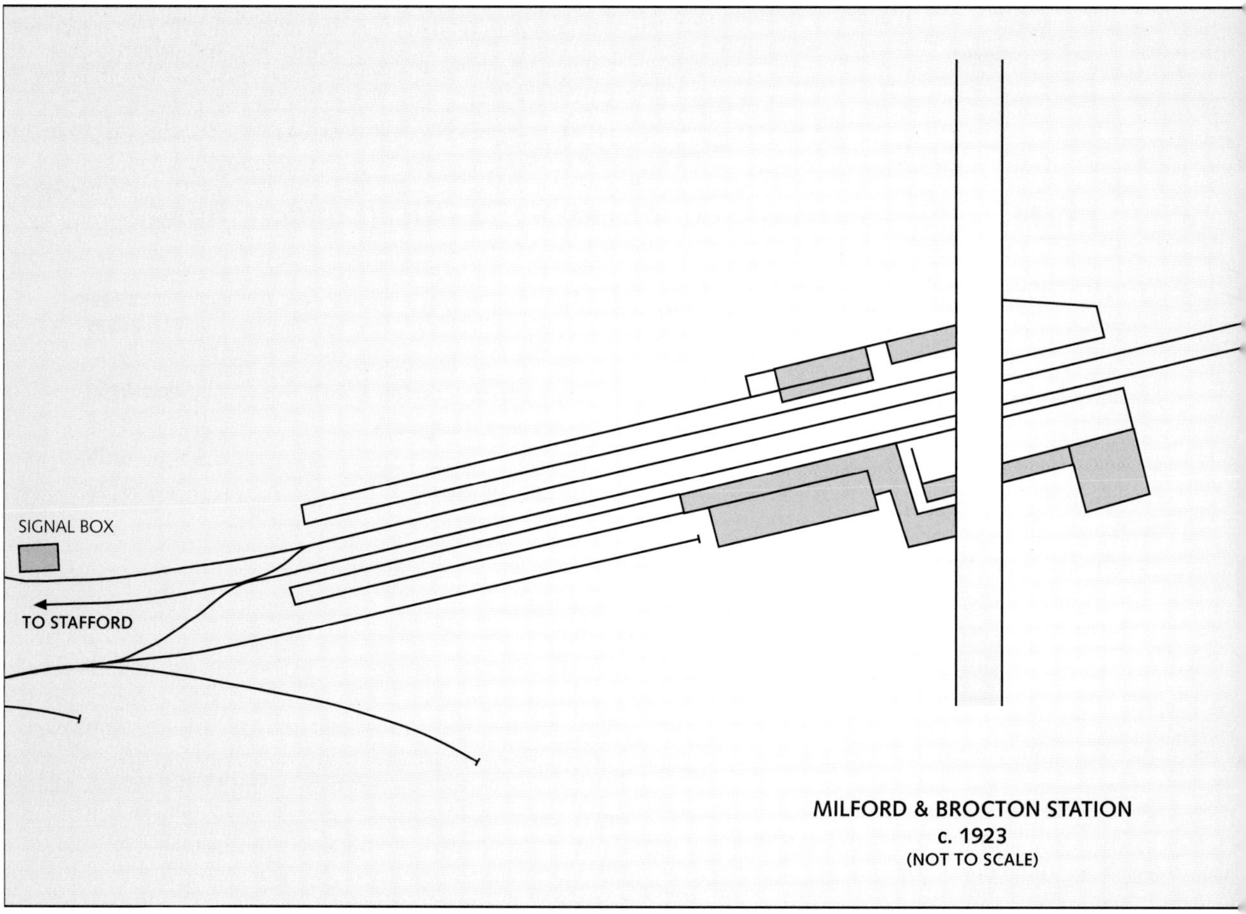

SIGNAL BOX

TO STAFFORD

MILFORD & BROCTON STATION
c. 1923
(NOT TO SCALE)

Milford and Brocton station, *c.* 1905. The station here was opened to passengers on 18 May 1877 and to goods on 22 January 1882. This view is looking south towards Shugborough Tunnel from the Down platform and shows the road overbridge that gave access to the short wooden platforms. The station buildings were also constructed in timber and were single-storey affairs of simple design. The small goods siding was behind the Down platform. The line between here and Stafford was quadrupled in 1898, opening on 26 July of that year. The station here survived until 6 March 1950, when it was closed to passengers. Goods traffic lasted for another decade, the station closing to freight on 7 March 1960. *(Author's Collection)*

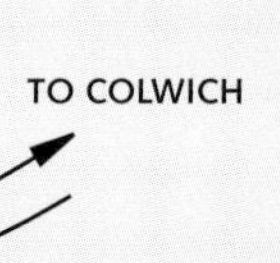

A plan of Milford and Brocton station. *c.* 1923. *(Author)*

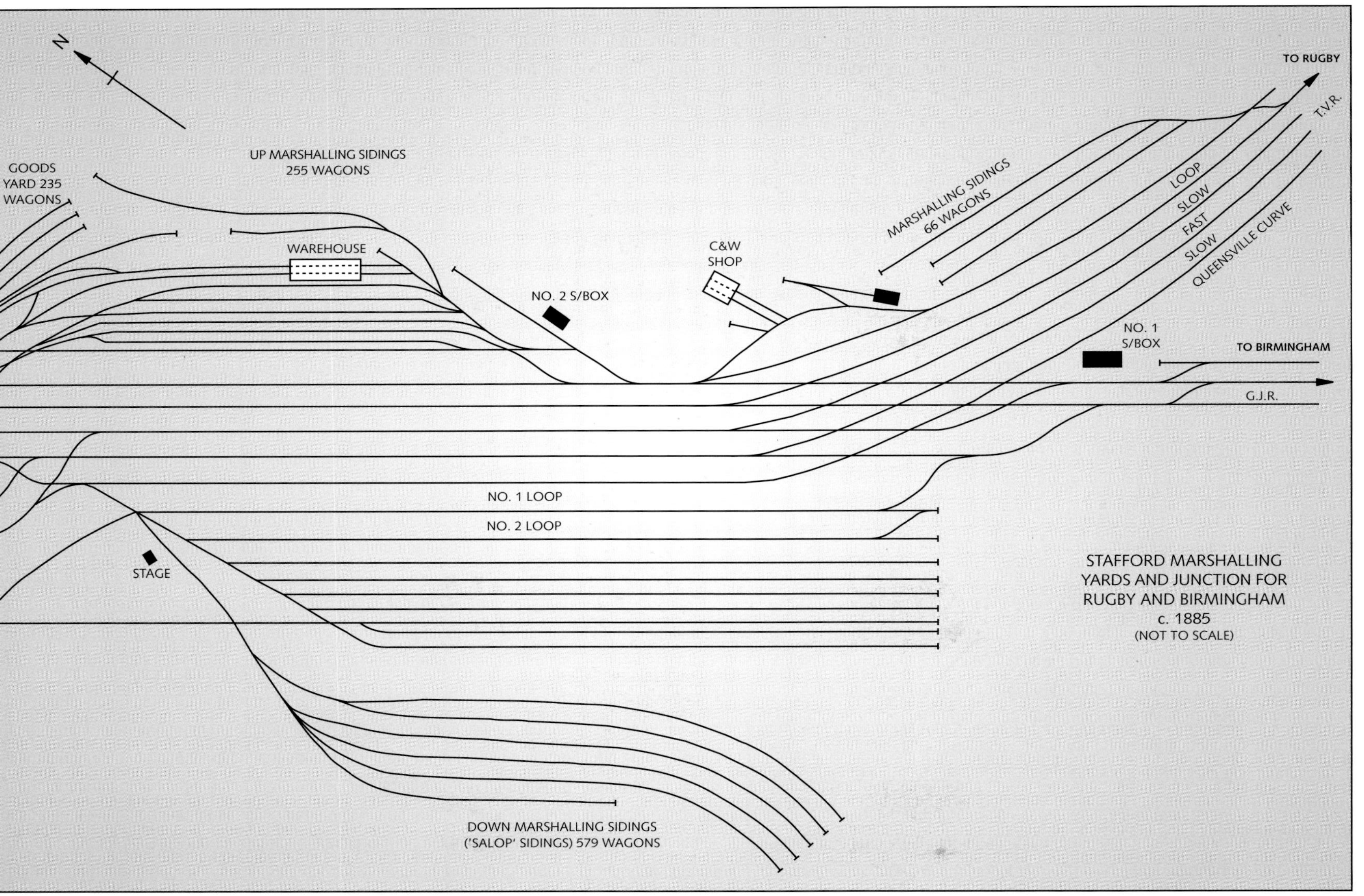

A plan of the southern end of Stafford station, showing the entrance to the Queensville Curve and the TVR. *(Author)*

These railway cottages, pictured in 1974, were built by the LNWR for station staff at Milford and Brocton. Like many built by the railway company, they were built of bricks made in the LNWR brickworks at Crewe. *(D. Ibbotson)*

The TVR ends at Stafford and the station is approached via the tight Queensville Curve. This 25-chain curve was so tight that a speed restriction of 30mph was imposed. In 1938, with the introduction of the high-speed 'Coronation-Scot', Queensville Curve was realigned to increase speeds to 55mph. To do this, the junction with the GJR at Stafford was relaid, with two level chairs and switch diamonds installed. The less important GJR line to Birmingham was realigned with permitted speeds remaining at 30mph. Queensville Curve was slewed by up to 11ft 7in and given an additional cant. The scheme cost £8,000 for new track and £2,000 for track alterations. This view shows a southbound train leaving Stafford and heading for the TVR over the old Queensville Curve in about 1905. On the right is the GJR line for Birmingham. *(F.W. Shuttleworth Collection)*

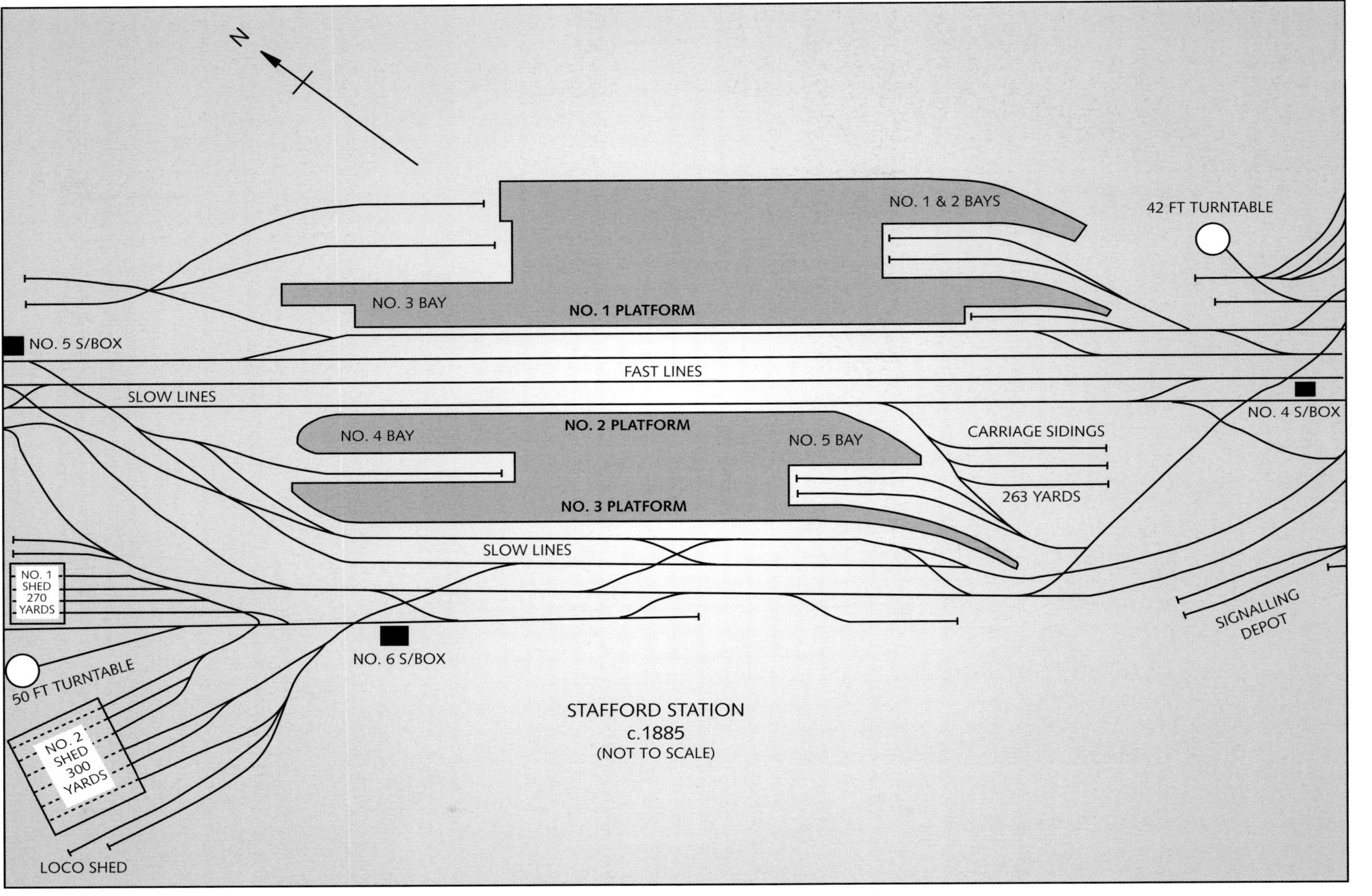

A plan of the main station area at Stafford, *c.* 1885. The original GJR station here survived until 1844, when it was replaced by a new one, designed by John Cunningham of Liverpool in Elizabethan style. However, it soon became clear that this station was also inadequate and a brand new station in 'Euston style' was opened in 1861, a little distance north of the previous one. This station, with extra trackwork for avoiding lines, which created a new island platform, is shown here. *(Author)*

Pictured at Stafford is LNWR 'Dreadnought' 2–2–2–0 compound no. 510 *Leviathan* at the head of a Euston-bound express. In LNWR days Anglo-Scottish expresses called at Stafford where passengers could obtain luncheon baskets. *(R. Carpenter)*

Another 'Dreadnought' locomotive no. 321 *Servia* waits at Stafford station, having just left the TVR with a Down train in 1904. *(R. Carpenter)*

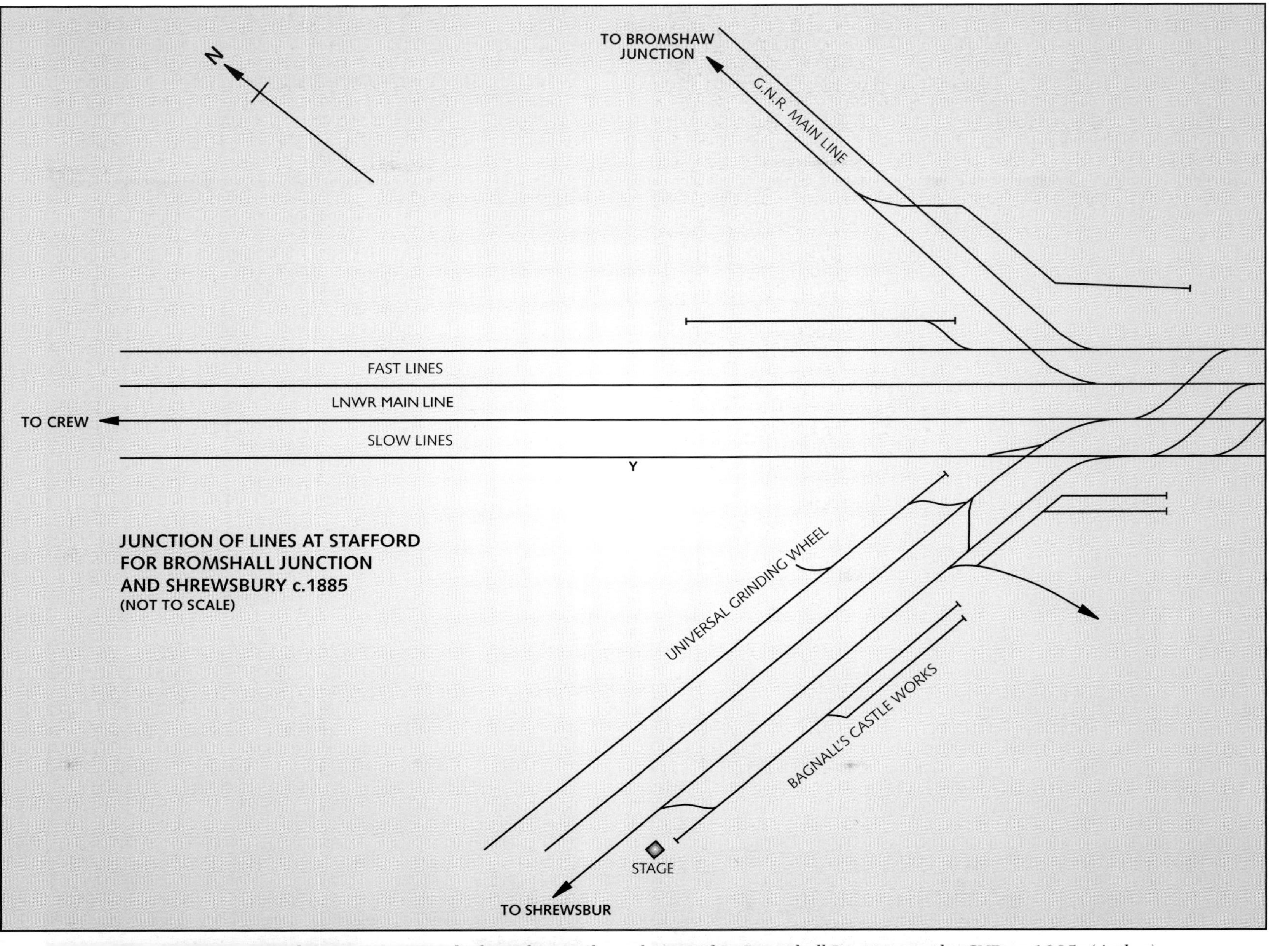
TO BROMSHAW
JUNCTION
G.N.R. MAIN LINE
N
FAST LINES
LNWR MAIN LINE
TO CREW
SLOW LINES
Y
JUNCTION OF LINES AT STAFFORD
FOR BROMSHALL JUNCTION
AND SHREWSBURY c.1885
(NOT TO SCALE)
UNIVERSAL GRINDING WHEEL
BAGNALL'S CASTLE WORKS
STAGE
TO SHREWSBUR

Hauling the Up 'Midday Scot' from Glasgow to Euston, via the TVR, through Stafford is ex-LMS 'Princess-Coronation' Pacific no. 46229 *Duchess of Hamilton* on 6 May 1959. *(R. Carpenter)*

The Up 'Red Rose' from Liverpool to Euston, with ex-LMS 'Black 5' 4–6–0 no. 44907 and ex-LMS 'Patriot' 4–6–0 no. 45551 in charge, enters Stafford station on 6 May 1959. *(R. Carpenter)*

Ex-LMS 'Princess-Coronation' Pacific no. 46248 *City of Leeds* approaching Stafford no. 5 signal-box as it heads an express for Euston. *(R. Carpenter)*

Ex-LMS Stanier 2–6–2 tank locomotive no. 40122 on station pilot duties at Stafford in the late 1950s. *(R. Carpenter)*

Just north of Stafford station lay the site of Bagnall's locomotive works. The company was established in 1875 and produced railway locomotives, wagons, track and complete railways which were sent all over the British Empire as well as serving British industrial railway networks. The company also built engines for the GWR, LMS, and Somerset & Dorset Joint Railway. Here, Stafford-built locomotives await export to the Indian subcontinent. The chimneys of the locoworks can be seen on the right. *(Allan Baker)*

W. G. BAGNALL, LD.,

Castle Engine Works, STAFFORD.

MAKERS OF

Locomotives

FOR ALL GAUGES,

Portable and Light Railways, Sleepers, Carriages, Wagons, Tip Trucks, Switches, Chilled Wheels, Turntables,

&c.

Plantation Rolling Stock.

PATENT TIPPING WAGONS OF NEW DESIGN, being the best and strongest offered, at lowest prices. Kept in stock.

WORKS LAID OUT WITH NARROW GAUGE SYSTEMS.

Small Locomotives are kept in Stock, of first-class material and Workmanship, which will compete in price with those of any other known maker.

Telegraphic Address—"BAGNALL, STAFFORD." Telephone 15. Codes—Engineering, A B C.

An advertisement for Bagnall's. The works here eventually closed, under GEC, in 1972. Over the years the works had provided skilled employment for hundreds of people in Stafford and many of its products would have been transported over the TVR for onward shipment abroad. *(Author's Collection)*

TRENT VALLEY RAILWAY STATIONS

Distance	*Station*	*Opened*	*Closed*	*Comments*
0	Rugby	1838 (as part of L&B)		New station opened in 1886
5½ miles	Brinklow	1 Dec 1847	14 Sept 1957	Originally named 'Stretton' until 1 Feb 1870. Closed to freight 20 Feb 1961.
3¼ miles	Shilton	1 Dec 1847	14 Sept 1957	Closed to freight 1965.
2¼ miles	Bulkington	1 Dec 1847	18 May 1931	Saxby & Farmer signal-box closed in 1936 and replaced by LNWR Type 5 box.
3½ miles	Nuneaton	15 Sept 1847		Station rebuilt to First Class standard 1913–15. Station renamed Nuneaton (Trent Valley) 2 June 1924. Closed to freight 1965.
5½ miles	Atherstone	15 Sept 1847 (First Class station)		Interior modernised in 1902. Closed to freight May 1964. Became unmanned station in autumn 1972.
4 miles	Polesworth	15 Sept 1947		Became unmanned station in autumn 1972.
3½ miles	Tamworth	15 Sept 1847 (First Class station)		Exchange point for mail trains until 6 March 1967. New station opened 24 Sept 1962.
6¼ miles	Lichfield	15 Sept 1847 (First Class station)		New station opened 3 March 1871.
4¾ miles	Armitage	15 Sept 1847	13 June 1960	Opened to goods traffic 1 October 1877 and closed in May 1964.
3¼ miles	Rugeley	15 Sept 1847		Renamed Rugeley (Trent Valley) 15 April 1917. Closed to freight in May 1964. Became unmanned station in autumn 1972.
2¾ miles	Colwich	15 Sept 1847	14 Sept 1957	Junction with NSR Colwich–Stone line from 1 May 1849. New station opened in 1871.
3¼ miles	Milford and Brocton	18 May 1877	6 March 1950	Closed to freight traffic 7 March 1960.
3¼ miles	Stafford	4 July 1837 (as part of GJR)		New station opened in 1861. Completely rebuilt as part of WCML electrification 31 December 1962.

51 miles total distance

Junctions with The Trent Valley Railway

Rugby	The London & Birmingham Railway opened 9 April 1838. LNWR opened 1 March 1851, closed 15 June 1959	Birmingham–London (Euston) Rugby-Leamington Spa
Nuneaton	South Leicestershire Railway opened 1 January 1864, became part of LNWR on 15 July 1867	Nuneaton–Leicester
	LNWR Nuneaton loop for line to Coventry opened 1 January 1864	Nuneaton–Coventry
	Midland Railway opened 12 September 1850, closed 18 January 1969. Reopened in the late 1970s.	Nuneaton–Whitacre
	Ashby and Nuneaton, NR/LNWR joint line opened in 1873, closed in 1971	Nuneaton–Burton-on-Trent
	Spur opened between LNWR and MR opened in 1880	Nuneaton (Trent Valley) to Nuneaton (Abbey Street)
Tamworth	Birmingham & Derby Junction Railway (became part of Midland Railway from 10 May 1844) opened 12 August 1839	Birmingham (Hampton-in-Arden)–Derby
Lichfield	South Staffordshire Railway (LNWR) opened 3 November 1884 and closed 18 January 1965. Section between Birmingham and Lichfield (City) now used as part of the suburban 'Cross City' service between Redditch, Birmingham (New Street) and Lichfield	Birmingham–Derby
Rugeley	South Staffordshire Railway line serving coalfields in the Cannock area. Opened 1 August 1850 and closed 18 January 1965	Rugeley–Walsall
Colwich	North Staffordshire Railway opened 1 May 1849. Local trains ceased in 1947, but line remained to be electrified, completed on 6 March 1967	Colwich–Stone
Stafford	Grand Jubilee Railway, opened 4 July 1837	Birmingham–Earlestown

Companies Served by the TVR

Several private companies had sidings with connections to the Trent Valley Railway, providing a great deal of freight traffic for the line and the railway company. Most of these sidings had disappeared by the 1960s, owing to closure or transfer to road transport.

Company	*Industry*	*Comments*
B.T. Forder & Son Ltd, Bulkington	Stone quarries	Sidings situated 1,150 yards north of Bulkington station, opened 27 March 1904, and controlled by a ground frame. The sidings were closed in 1938.
Attleborough Quarries (owned by Foxwell & Davies from 1874), Nuneaton	Stone quarries	Sidings situated south of Nuneaton; became disused during the first two decades of the twentieth century.
Sterling Metals Ltd, Nuneaton	Aircraft and automotive parts manufacturer	Sidings opened on 19 September 1955 and went out of use in the late 1960s.
Swinnerton's Timber Yard, Nuneaton	Timber producers	Sidings opened with the TVR, the yard having been used by the line's contractors, building and repairing ballast wagons as well as providing timber for construction of the line. Wagons continued to be repaired here for over forty years. The sidings were closed in the 1960s, after being a source of local railway traffic for many years.
Nuneaton & Chilvers UDC Sewage Works Siding	Sewage works	Siding to accommodate six trucks provided into the sewage works in 1895 from the LNWR goods yard.
Jee's Quarry (established in 1822), Hartshill, Nuneaton	Stone quarries	Sidings opened with the TVR. The railway system was abandoned in October 1954, all signs of its existence being destroyed by extensive quarrying.
Mancetter & Abell Granite Quarries, Hartshill and Mancetter (between Nuneaton and Atherstone)	Stone quarries	Sidings opened in the 1880s. The railway system was abandoned in April 1956. The ground frame at Mancetter was electrically released from Atherstone signal-box from 11 November 1962.
Atherstone Grain Silo (built by the Ministry of Agriculture, Fisheries and Food in 1943–4)	Grain silo	Sidings were adjacent to Atherstone station, with connection to the TVR on the Down side. Rail traffic ceased in the early 1970s.

Baddesley Colliery, Atherstone	Coal mining	Sidings opened close to Coventry Canal wharf in 1871 and closed in the 1970s.
Pooley Hall Colliery, Polesworth	Coal mining	Sidings opened 1896. Amington colliery, opened in 1862, merged with Pooley Hall in 1951 and surface workings were maintained until 1963. The colliery officially closed on 16 April 1965.
Glascote Colliery, Tamworth	Coal mining	Sidings were opened in 1862. The pit closed in 1943 and the rail system was abandoned in June 1951.
Tamworth Colliery Co., Tamworth	Coal mining	Sidings (Marshalls Siding) opened on 29 October 1877 and closed in 1951.
Alders of Tamworth	Paper manufacturers (since 1810)	Sidings were opened at the end of March 1927, half a mile north of Tamworth station. These were run down from May 1967, and BR officially closed them in October 1967.
Trent Valley Brewery Co. Ltd, Lichfield	Beer brewers (founded December 1875)	Double siding opened in 1875.
Rom River Reinforcement Ltd, Lichfield	Concrete producers	Sidings opened in 1963, on the Down side of the TVR.
Armitage Sanitary Works, Armitage	Sanitary ware manufacturers (now known as Armitage-Shanks Ltd)	Sidings opened in October 1877. (Railwaymen knew it as 'Toilet Basin Junction'!)
Colwich Brick & Tile Co., Colwich	Brick and tile manufacturers	Sidings existed on the Up side, close to Colwich station, and were controlled by a ground frame. The sidings went out of use in the early 1950s.
Cannock Chase Camp Military Railway		Opened in 1915 to a connection with the TVR on the Down side of Milford and Brocton station. It closed in 1919.
Stafford Salt & Alkali Co., Baswich	Salt producers	Private siding controlled by a ground frame. It closed in the mid-1950s.
British Reinforced Concrete Engineering Co. Ltd, Stafford	Concrete producers	Works established in the mid-1920s, with sidings on the Down side of the TVR by Queensville signal-box. These sidings were closed in the 1980s.

EXPRESS TRAINS OPERATING OVER THE TRENT VALLEY RAILWAY IN 1955

The 1950s were the peak years for railway travel and 1955 was the last year of full steam haulage before the introduction of diesel traction the following year. The number of express services over the TVR in 1955 shows just how busy the line was. Several different locosheds supplied motive power for these services, as shown here.

Up Depart	*Down Depart*	*Train*	*Locomotive*	*Shed*
	00.20	Euston–Glasgow	Princess-Coronation	1B
	00.30	Euston–Liverpool	Princess-Royal	8A
	00.40	Euston–Manchester	Jubilee	8A
20.50		Crewe–Euston (Parcels)	Royal Scot	5A
21.50		Liverpool–Euston (Parcels)	Princess-Royal	8A
22.33		Manchester–Euston (Parcels)	Royal Scot/Britannia	9A
20.30		Windermere–Euston	Royal Scot	1B
18.25		Glasgow/Aberdeen–Euston (TPO)	Royal Scot	5A
18.35		Kendal–Euston (Parcels)	Royal Scot	5A
17.40		Glasgow–Euston	Royal Scot	1B
00.02		Manchester–Euston	Royal Scot/Britannia	9A
00.10		Liverpool–Euston	Royal Scot	8A
01.10		Holyhead–Euston	Royal Scot/Britannia	6J
21.27		Glasgow–Euston	Princess-Coronation	12B
22.20		Glasgow–Euston	Princess-Coronation	1B
20.15		Perth–Euston	Royal Scot	1B
22.25		Glasgow–Euston	Princess-Coronation	1B
	07.55	Euston–Liverpool	Princess-Coronation	1B
22.00		Stranraer–Euston	Royal Scot	1B
17.15		Inverness–Euston	Princess-Coronation	5A
	08.30	Euston–Manchester	Royal Scot/Britannia	9A
	09.45	Euston–Manchester	Royal Scot/Britannia	9A
	10.00	Euston–Glasgow	Princess-Coronation	1B
	10.40	Euston–Carlisle	Princess-Coronation	1B
	10.50	Euston–Blackpool	Royal Scot	1B
07.48		Crewe–Euston	Princess-Coronation	5A
08.00		Manchester–Euston	Royal Scot/Britannia	9A

Up Depart	*Down Depart*	*Train*	*Locomotive*	*Shed*
07.00		Heysham–Euston	Royal Scot	1B
	11.45	Euston–Manchester	Royal Scot/Britannia	9A
08.10		Liverpool–Euston	Princess-Royal	8A
	12.30	Euston–Liverpool	Princess-Royal	8A
08.20		Manchester–Euston	Royal Scot/Britannia	9A
08.00		Blackpool–Euston	Royal Scot	1B
09.45		Manchester–Euston	Royal Scot/Britannia	9A
07.30		Holyhead–Euston	Royal Scot/Britannia	6J
	13.30	Euston–Glasgow	Princess-Coronation	5A
	13.35	Euston–Blackpool	Jubilee	24E
10.10		Liverpool–Euston	Princess-Royal	8A
10.05		Manchester–Euston	Royal Scot/Britannia	9A
	14.30	Euston–Liverpool	Royal Scot	8A
	14.45	Euston–Manchester	Royal Scot/Britannia	9A
11.10		Liverpool–Euston	Jubilee	8A
10.00		Blackpool–Euston	Royal Scot	1B
09.10		Llandudno–Euston	Jubilee	5A
	15.45	Euston–Manchester	Royal Scot/Britannia	9A
12.05		Manchester–Euston	Jubilee	9A
08.30		Carlisle–Euston	Royal Scot	1B
	16.30	Euston–Manchester	Royal Scot	1B
	16.55	Euston–Liverpool	Royal Scot	8A
	17.05	Euston–Blackpool	Royal Scot	1B
10.00		Glasgow–Euston	Princess-Coronation	1B
	17.35	Euston–Holyhead	Royal Scot	5A
14.10		Liverpool–Euston	Royal Scot	8A
14.05		Manchester–Euston	Royal Scot/Britannia	9A
	18.00	Euston–Manchester	Royal Scot/Britannia	9A
	18.10	Euston–Liverpool	Princess-Royal	8A
	18.20	Euston–Heysham	Royal Scot	1B
	18.30	Euston–Preston	Princess-Coronation	5A

Up Depart	*Down Depart*	*Train*	*Locomotive*	*Shed*
	19.20	Euston–Inverness	Royal Scot	1B
09.00		Perth–Euston	Princess-Coronation	1B
	19.30	Euston–Perth	Princess-Coronation	1B
16.05		Manchester–Euston	Royal Scot/Britannia	9A
16.10		Liverpool–Euston	Royal Scot	8A
	20.30	Euston–Glasgow/Aberdeen (TPO)	Princess-Coronation	5A
	20.50	Euston–Holyhead	Royal Scot/Britannia	6J
17.25		Liverpool–Euston	Princess-Coronation	1B
13.30		Glasgow–Euston	Princess-Coronation	1B
	21.10	Euston–Glasgow	Princess-Coronation	1B
17.50		Manchester–Euston	Royal Scot/Britannia	9A
	21.25	Euston–Glasgow	Princess-Coronation	12B
	22.00	Euston–Manchester (Parcels)	Royal Scot/Britannia	9A
	22.45	Euston–Manchester	Royal Scot/Britannia	9A
	22.52	Euston–Perth	Royal Scot/Britannia	6J
17.05		Blackpool–Euston	Jubilee	24E
	23.05	Euston–Windermere	Jubilee	5A
	23.50	Euston–Glasgow (St Enoch)	Royal Scot	1B

TOTAL: 76 (average 3.17 trains per hour over the TVR)

SHED CODES

1B – Camden
5A – Crewe North
6J – Holyhead
8A – Liverpool Edge Hill
9A – Manchester Longsight
12B – Carlisle Upperby
24E – Blackpool

2

The Locosheds

In LMS days long-distance expresses operating over the TVR were hauled by Pacific or 4–6–0 locomotives from Camden or Crewe North sheds. Until then, most trains over the TVR were in the charge of engines provided by locosheds at Stafford, Nuneaton and Rugby. Stafford and Rugby sheds were at each end of the line, while Nuneaton shed was about halfway along. The most important of these three sheds was Rugby, where the nearby station was at various times the engine changing point for several services, particularly Liverpool/Manchester–Euston expresses in the 1870s. Rugby was also an important and complex junction, making it an obvious site for the establishment of an engine shed, along with servicing facilities.

At the other end of the TVR there was a smaller and less important locoshed at Stafford. Its history as a locomotive stabling point dated back to the opening of the Grand Junction Railway in 1837, but no shed building existed there until the 1850s, after Richard Trevithick, chief mechanical engineer at Crewe, had made several requests for a shed at Stafford. Despite all of his efforts, the Locomotive Committee only approved construction in 1852, and a shed holding twelve locomotives was built soon afterwards.

The only locoshed actually on the TVR was at Nuneaton. Engines had been stabled there since before 1855, when 'Coventry and Nuneaton' was listed as having three engines (two in steam and one spare). A small depot existed at Nuneaton before 1870, it being a sub-shed of Rugby for many years. It was little used, however, and part was rented out to contractors working on the Trent Valley line.

All three sheds went on to provide locomotives for many local and freight trains which ran over the TVR, although their role in the provision of top-link express engines had diminished substantially by the beginning of the twentieth century. Modernisation in the 1960s spelt the end for these locosheds as the new diesel and electric traction required much less maintenance than did steam and therefore fewer locomotives were required to operate train services. Thus all three locosheds had disappeared by the end of the 1960s.

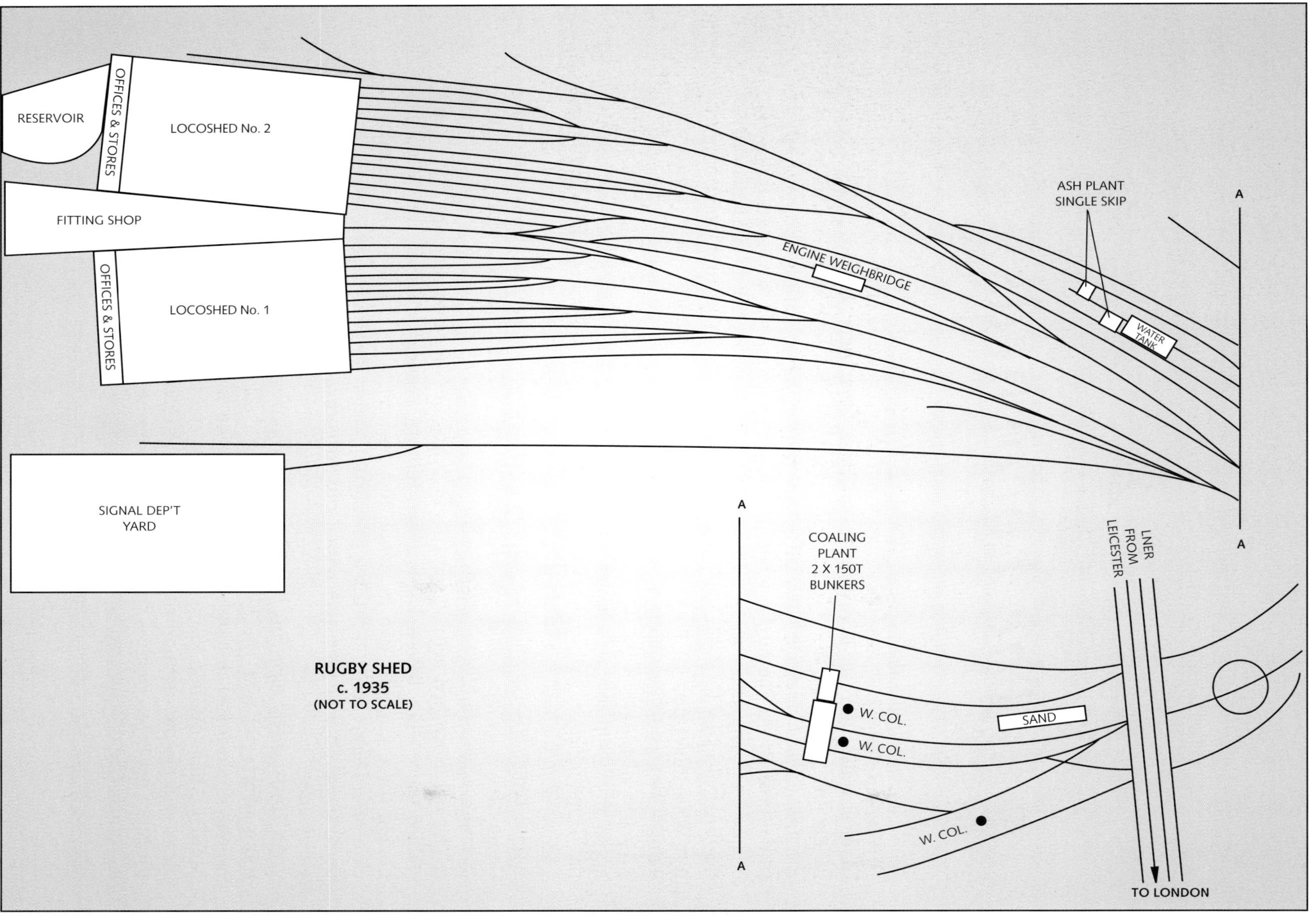

A plan of the large and important shed at Rugby, showing the two sheds that existed there. *(Author)*

Ex-Midland Railway 0–6–0 no. 3691 outside Rugby shed on 27 August 1938. As early as 1847 it was realised that extensive locomotive accommodation was required at Rugby and in 1850 J.E. McConnell, chief mechanical engineer at Wolverton, reported that additional shelter for engines was 'much required at Rugby', there being 22 engines in steam daily but only shed room for 11. He proposed a shed 'like the one to be erected at Bletchley'. A new shed was built in the following year and by 1853 two sheds were in use, one for the northern and the other for the southern division. By 1866 there were 100 locomotives at Rugby, 39 passenger types (including 5 bankers) and 54 goods engines, along with 5 shunters, and a couple of 'ballast engines'. Water for the locomotives came from the River Avon at this time, but the supply was rather irregular. To overcome this problem, Ramsbottom, who was now CME of the LNWR, suggested the construction of a 500,000-gallon reservoir, a proposal which was approved by the Locomotive Committee. The following year an extra siding was installed to prevent locomotives having to approach or leave the turntable by the same road, a practice that could be 'very dangerous in foggy weather'. Material for the siding was to be obtained from the 'Peterborough Coke Oven Sidings'. In 1875 the whole system was ordered to be moved 'to a new position on the Stamford line'. The first shed was completed the following year and by 1866 two large straight sheds, identical in size and appearance, had been erected at the north side of the station. Both had northlight pattern roofs, with a large LNWR coal stage and water tank above. Two 40-ft turntables were provided in the yard. A three-road repair shop, which was an outstation of Crewe, was established on the site to the north. By 1909 the shed, which had the LNWR code no. 8, was very extensive and 160 engines were based there, including '26 of the newest Precursor 4–4–0s'. At this time nearly 900 men were employed there, and six sub-sheds, at Warwick, Coventry, Peterborough, Stamford, Seaton and Market Harborough, made Rugby one of the most important sheds on the LNWR system. *(L. Hanson)*

Ex-LNWR Webb 2–4–0 no. 5000 *Princess Beatrice* at Rugby shed, February 1932. By 1935 Rugby was the chief depot of a large district, receiving LMS code 2A, and a number of improvements were carried out. New coal and ash plants were built by Mitchell Engineering and Dempster & Sons in 1934, and between 1938 and 1943 many pits were altered and renewed at a cost of £3,000. No. 1 shed, the nearest to the station, was designated a sub-depot under the LMS 1933 scheme, and no. 2 became a 'concentration' depot. A 55-ft turntable was installed at the far end of the yard, beyond a viaduct carrying GCR tracks over the West Coast Main Line. *(Author's Collection)*

Ex-LNWR 'Precursor' 4–4–0 no. 5300 *Hydra* at Rugby shed in 1933. Express locomotive changing at Rugby was abandoned by the LMS, and this left Rugby shed as a home for freight engines, and express types were rarely allocated until the mass withdrawals of the 1960s consigned 'Jubilee' and 'Patriot' 4–6–0s to lesser duties. Its position on an important junction, however, ensured that the shed remained one of the more important depots on the LMS and it received a large collection of new Stanier locomotives when they came into service. Some 40 'Black 5' 4–6–0s were allocated in 1954, along with 10 8F 2–8–0s. The remaining allocation at this time consisted of 10 LNWR 0–8–0s 2–6–4 tanks, ex M.R. and LMS 4F 0–6–0s, 3F 0–6–0 tanks and 4P 4–4–0s. One of Webb's 2–4–2 tanks, no. 46604 was also allocated to Rugby. *(Author's Collection)*

One of Rugby shed's allocation of 4P 4–4–0s, no. 41122, being steamed on 11 April 1954. By the end of the Second World War, the shed roofs had become untidy, owing to lack of attention by the LMS. In 1955 no. 1 shed was largely demolished, and a new higher roof, in steel with corrugated sheeting, was provided, the building having been drastically shortened at the same time. No. 2 shed was scheduled for the same treatment but was left untouched, and finally demolished in 1960 to make way for a car park. The works closed in 1959, but was subsequently used as a fitting shop for new BTH/BRCW electric locomotives. *(R. Carpenter)*

Ex-LNWR Webb 2–4–2 tank locomotive no. 46604 at Rugby shed on 11 April 1954. *(R. Carpenter)*

Ex-LNWR 8F 0–8–0 no. 49112 at Rugby shed on 11 April 1954. These engines were the mainstay of heavy freight haulage for many years at Rugby shed and were used on the heavy coal trains which emanated from the collieries situated all the way along the TVR. *(R. Carpenter)*

Another ex-LNWR 0–8–0, no. 48914, at Rugby shed on 11 April 1954. In 1958/9 a repair shop was built between the two sheds for the 12 diesel shunters then based at Rugby, but advancing electrification finally saw off the depot and it closed, along with Crewe North, on 24 April 1963. The shed ended its life coded 1F. The no. 1 shed building was used as a stock store and diesel shunter stabling point after closure, but it has since been demolished and no trace of it now remains. *(R. Carpenter)*

A general view of Nuneaton shed, with several locomotives in steam on 8 August 1953. Following the opening of the TVR, sufficient extra traffic was generated for Francis Webb to propose a new locoshed at Nuneaton which was to hold 12 engines. Approval was given in 1878 and the shed was opened in the same year. It was erected in the fork between the branch to Coventry and the TVR, and was in contemporary LNWR style with, at first, a 42-ft turntable. Nuneaton shed was doubled in size in 1888, and enlarged again in 1897 by extending the shed some 90ft in the rear. Other improvements were carried out at the same time, including the provision of a larger 50-ft turntable a few yards south of the original, new offices were built at the rear of the shed, and an extra siding. The small original coal stage at the north end of the yard was replaced by a much larger one at 'Mill Sidings' near the Coventry line. Nuneaton grew rapidly into a very busy depot, primarily concerned with freight, mostly coal, and had a large allocation of LNWR 0–6–0s and 0–6–2 coal tanks. By 1925 the shed, LNWR code 4, had an allocation of 70 locomotives, with a further 8 at four sub-sheds in Coalville, Loughborough, Overseal and the ex-MR shed at Leicester. The allocation had increased to over 80 by 1939, of which nearly half were ex-LNWR 0–8–0s. Several new 2–6–2 tanks, used on secondary passenger services, were also allocated to Nuneaton. During the Leicester holiday weeks Nuneaton supplied motive power and men for at least part of the journeys of some fifty excursions. Under BR auspices the size of Nuneaton's allocation was largely maintained, with 8Fs replacing 0–8–0s and Ivatt 43xxx moguls replacing the ageing 0–6–0s. *(Author's Collection)*

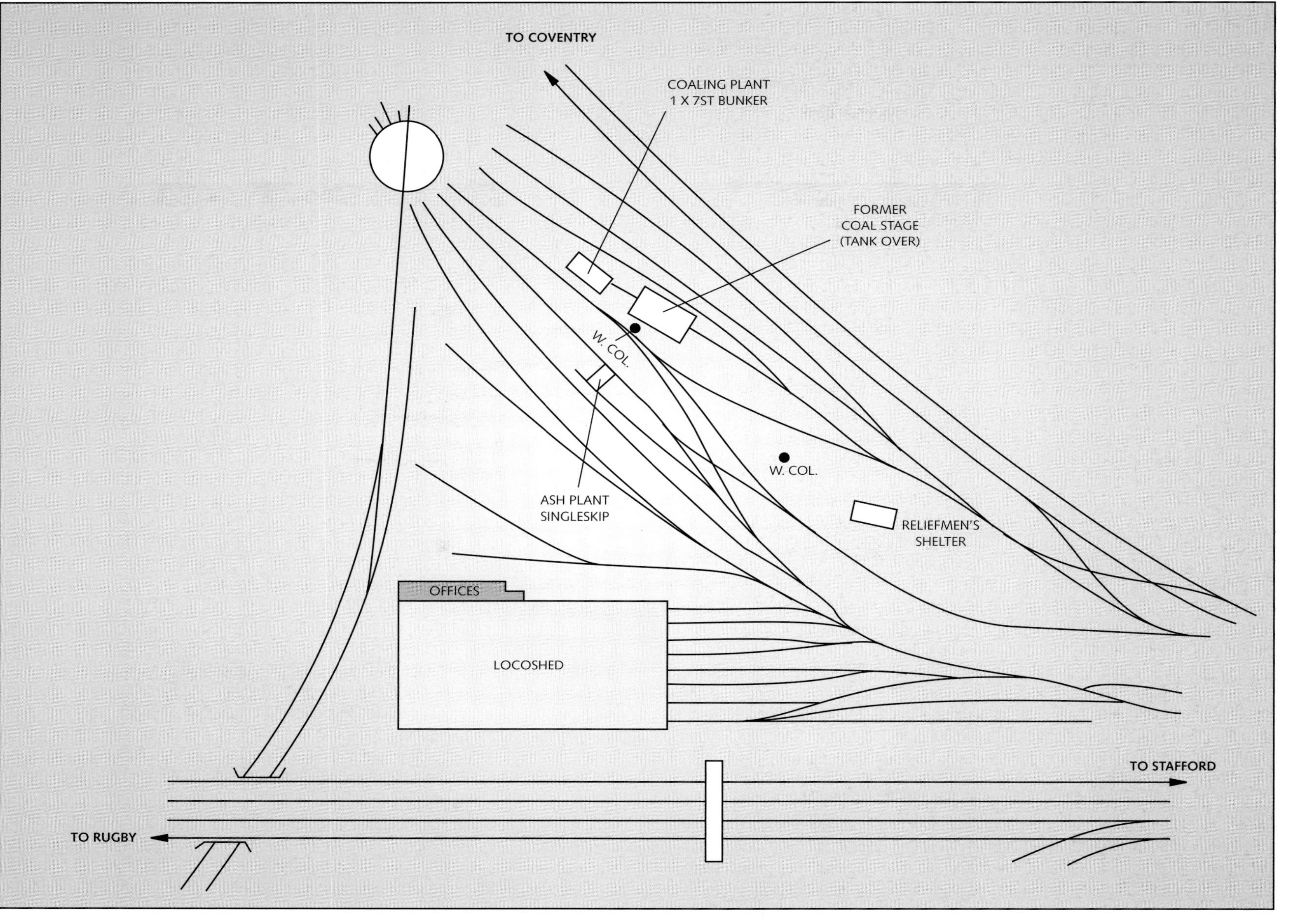

A plan of Nuneaton shed, situated on the junction between the TVR and the branch to Coventry. *(Author)*

Ex-LNWR Class B four-cylinder 0–8–0 no. 1282 at Nuneaton shed in 1925. The sub-sheds of Nuneaton all disappeared in the 1930s and Nuneaton was re-coded 2D in 1935, becoming 2B after nationalisation. The shed finished life as 5E from September 1963. The LMS supplied coal and ash plants in 1936/7 and also installed a water softener. The turntable was replaced by a vacuum-operated 60ft unit in 1938, and the roof was renewed in BR days. *(R. Carpenter)*

Ex-LNWR 0–8–0 no. 49415 at Nuneaton shed on 1 November 1959. Nuneaton remained a very busy depot, handling more coal per day than the larger Rugby depot, the coaling plant often being overworked. Overcrowding became critical during the Second World War, when the yard was jammed with locomotives and delays occurred to engines leaving the shed. To relieve the situation in 1944, the LMS put in a new connection from the Leicester loop directly on to the new turntable. *(A.N.H. Glover)*

Ex-LMS 2–6–2 tank no. 40207, used on local passenger trains, pictured at Nuneaton shed on 1 November 1959. By this time the shed was nearing the end of its life. The last of its allocation of 0–8–0s left for Springs Branch in 1962, but the shed retained a large number of steam locomotives until the Crewe–Euston electrification sealed its fate a few years later. *(A.N.H. Glover)*

Ex-LMS 'Jinty' 0–6–0 tank no. 47594 at Nuneaton on 4 July 1952. In 1965 'Princess-Coronation' Pacific no. 46235 *City of Birmingham* was stored at Nuneaton shed en route to preservation at Birmingham Museum of Science and Industry. By this time there were very few steam turns at Nuneaton shed, and the last locomotive, 8F no. 48264, worked off shed on 4 June 1966, the depot closing two days later. It was soon demolished and no trace now remains. *(A.N.H. Glover)*

Stafford locoshed on 22 April 1962 with some of its allocation of 4–6–0s and tank locomotives. The opening of the TVR increased the importance of Stafford shed, and in 1860 the LNWR underwent some reorganisation, which made Stafford the limit of both its southern and northern divisions. As part of this process, an independent shed for the southern division was ordered to be built at Stafford, while the existing shed was to be extended. In April 1860 Mr Parnall, who had already built a number of sheds for the LNWR, was contracted to construct the new southern division shed at a price of £2,750 10*s*. The new shed was opened in the following year, built of brick with a hipped roof. It was provided with six roads and was later designated no. 2. The older four-road structure, which stood nearer the main line, was designated no. 1. Both sheds had offices and stores at the rear, with those of the older shed surmounted by a water tank. A 45-ft turntable, later enlarged to 50ft, was placed between the two sheds. At this time Stafford was at the height of its importance, and in the nineteenth century it was a very busy express locomotive depot. By the 1923 Grouping, the shed's importance had declined somewhat, and it had an allocation of only 40 engines. Stafford had no sub-sheds and carried the LNWR code 14, becoming 5O in 1935. By then the shed had become even less important, and its allocation had more than halved. Indeed, the shed had a surplus of space, most unusual at this time. In 1937/8 the turntable was enlarged to 60-ft and no. 1 shed, which was in a state of decay, was demolished, leaving only the offices and stores, along with the water tank at the rear. Coal and ash lifting apparatus, by Henry Lees & Co., was installed at the shed in the mid-1930s. A new roof was added to no. 2 shed in 1947, the shed finally closing on 19 July 1965. *(R. Carpenter)*

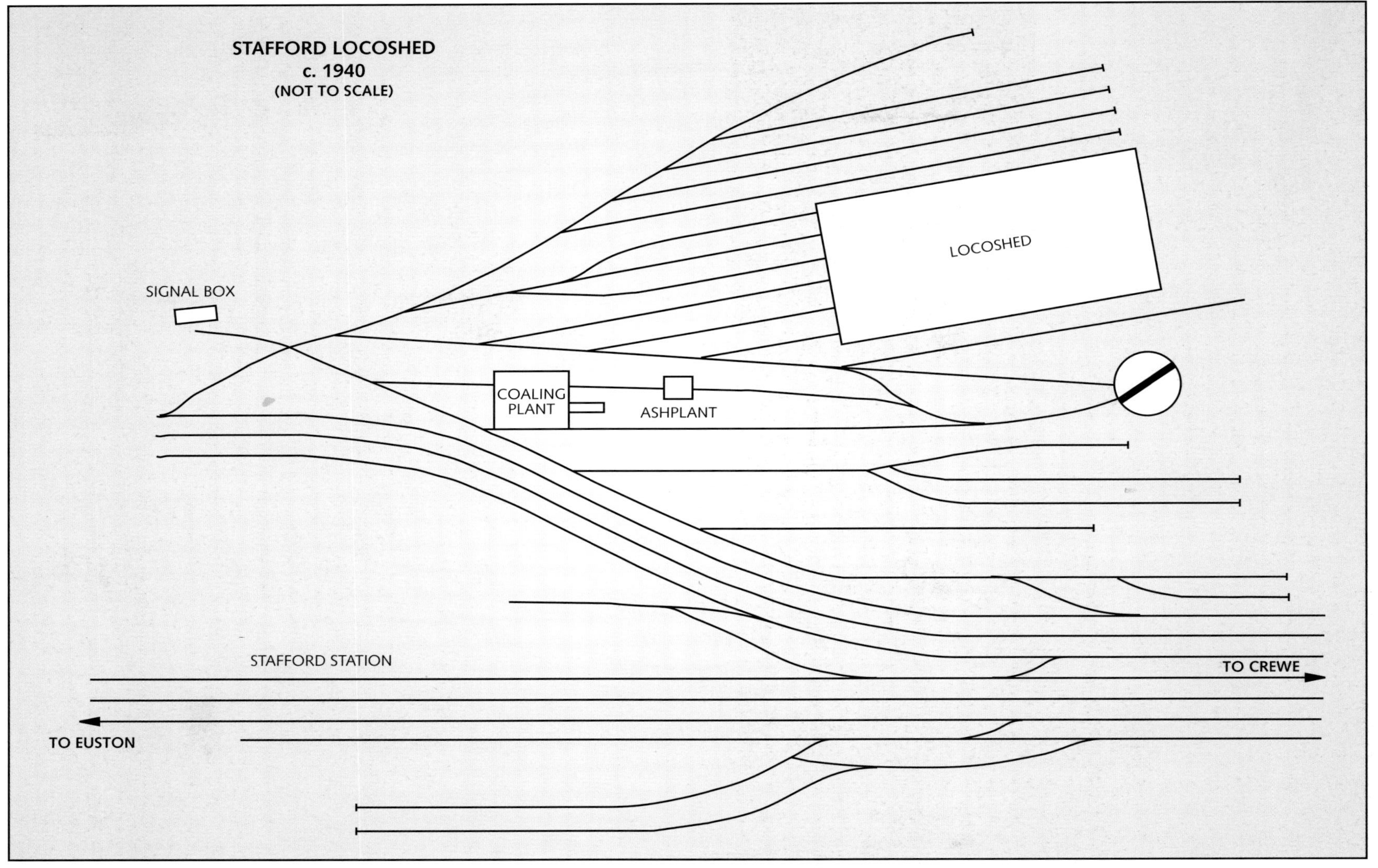

A plan of Stafford locoshed, *c.* 1940. *(Author)*

Ex-LNWR 0–6–0 'Special Tank' no. 7236 at Stafford shed in April 1933. *(Author's Collection)*

Ex-LNWR 'Precursor' 4–4–0 no. 5279 *Sunbeam* at Stafford shed in April 1933. *(Author's Collection)*

Ex-LNWR 18ft Goods 0–6–0 no. 8525 at Stafford shed in 1934. In its later years the shed's role was to supply locomotives for local passenger traffic and freight trains, this being reflected in its allocations. In the 1950s, several ex-LNWR 0–8–0 freight engines could be found there, but the last few had disappeared by the middle of the decade, along with a few 4–4–0s, 0–6–0 tanks and five 2–6–4 tanks. In 1960 these had given way to 8F 2–8–0s, 'Black 5' 4–6–0s and a few BR 'Standard' locomotives. Ex-LMS Fowler 2–6–4 tanks remained allocated to Stafford until 1964, nos 42309, 42389, and 42400 operating Shrewsbury passenger services. Shrewsbury-based engines operating similar services were serviced at Stafford, these usually being BR 'Standard' Class 5 4–6–0s or, on occasion, ex-LMS 'Jubilee' Class 4–6–0s. *(Author's Collection)*

Opposite: Ex-LMS 4F 0–6–0 no. 43948 at Stafford locoshed in the 1950s. Scenes like this are now just a distant memory since the disappearance of steam traction and the sheds which supplied the locomotives. *(R. Carpenter)*

Ex-LMS 4–6–2 tank locomotive no. 42389 rests at the coaling stage of Stafford shed in the late 1950s. These engines were used on local trains, some of which ran along the TVR. *(R. Carpenter)*

LOCOSHED ALLOCATIONS

RUGBY BR Code 2A (1F from 9 September 1963). Closed to steam 25 May 1965.

January 1957

LMS 4P 'Compound' 4–4–0	41105, 41113, 41122, 41162, 41165, 41172
LMS Class 2 2–6–2T	41214, 41278
LMS Class 4 2–6–4T	42061, 42062, 42489, 42541, 42573, 42576, 42577, 42585, 42615, 42669, 42673
LMS 4F 0–6–0	44064, 44395
LMS Class 5 4–6–0	44711, 44712, 44715, 44716, 44831, 44833, 44836, 44837, 44860, 44862, 44863, 44866, 44867, 44870, 44909, 44915, 45419, 45493
LMS 3F 'Jinty' 0–6–0T	47269, 47677
LMS 8F 2–8–0	48085, 48173, 48427, 48437, 48559, 48757
LNWR 7F 0–8–0	48914, 49049, 49114, 49245, 49249, 49377, 49397, 49405, 49413, 49417, 49433, 49435, 49452
MR 2F 0–6–0	58181, 58218, 58308

TOTAL: 63

September 1961

LMS Class 2 2–6–2T	41214
LMS Class 4 2–6–4T	42062, 42103, 42104, 42430, 42467, 42541, 42544, 42562, 42573, 42577, 42669
LMS Class 5 4–6–0	44711, 44712, 44715, 44716, 44760, 44771, 44831, 44833, 44836, 44860, 44862, 44863, 44866, 44870, 44897, 44909, 44915, 44938, 45050, 45056, 45513, 45130, 45139, 45222, 45419, 45493
LMS 'Jubilee' Class 4–6–0	45599 *Bechuanaland* 45603 *Solomon Islands* 45624 *St Helena* 45669 *Fisher* 45670 *Howard of Effingham* 45672 *Anson* 45684 *Jutland* 45704 *Leviathan* 45722 *Defence* 45733 *Novelty*
LMS 'Princess-Royal' Pacific	46206 *Princess Marie Louise*
LMS Class 2 2–6–0	46445, 46446
LMS 8F 2–8–0	48012, 48018, 48035, 48120, 48173, 48345, 48365, 48411, 48526, 48559

TOTAL: 61

May 1965 (Final allocation)

LMS Class 5 4–6–0	44715, 44716, 44771, 44831, 44836, 44866, 45001, 45065, 45113, 45448
LMS 8F 2–6–0	48005, 48365, 48445, 48526, 48559

TOTAL: 15

NUNEATON BR Code 2B (5E from 9 September 1963). Closed 6 June 1966.

January 1957

LMS Fowler Class 3 2–6–2T	40049
LMS Stanier Class 3 2–6–2T	40087, 40104, 40122, 40136, 40138, 40156, 40157, 40204, 40207
LMS Class 2 2–6–2T	41226, 41322, 41323
LMS Hughes 'Crab' 2-6–0	42781, 42783, 42817, 42854, 42891
LMS Class 4 2–6–0	43002, 43003, 43011, 43023, 43034
MR 3F 0–6–0	43308, 43786
LMS 4F 0–6–0	44157, 44292
LMS 'Jinty' 3F 0–6–0T	47285, 47286, 47492, 47594
LMS 8F 2–8–0	48016, 48020, 48077, 48154, 48258, 48312, 48320, 48343, 48345, 48372, 48398, 48435, 48449, 48456, 48526, 48658, 48686, 48716, 48723, 48751
LNWR 7F 0–8–0	48927, 49002, 49068, 49112, 49120, 49142, 49172, 49181, 49293, 49314, 49342, 49350, 49414, 49430, 49432
L&Y 3F 0–6–0	52201
MR 2F 0–6–0	58118

TOTAL: 68

September 1961

LMS Stanier Class 3 2–6–2T	40087, 40104, 40135, 40138, 40207
LMS Hughes 'Crab' 2–6–0	42781, 42783, 42811, 42926, 42933, 42939
LMS Stanier 6P5F 2–6–0	42945, 42951, 42953, 42954, 42955, 42960, 42964, 42965, 42975, 42976, 42978
LMS Class 4 2–6–0	43001, 43002, 43003, 43005, 43020, 43022, 43024, 43034
LMS 4F 0–6–0	43977
LMS 'Patriot' Class 4–6–0	45533 *Lord Rathmore* 45537 *Private E. Sykes VC* 45538 *Giggleswick* 45541 *Duke of Sutherland* 45542 45548 *Lytham St Annes*
LMS Class 2 2–6–0	46420, 46447
LMS 'Jinty' 3F 0–6–0T	47294, 47385, 47396, 47653

LMS 8F 2–8–0	48016, 48020, 48054, 48074, 48077, 48111, 48154, 48251, 48258, 48263, 48264, 48287, 48289, 48291, 48312, 48320, 48343, 48398, 48435, 48449, 48456, 48504, 48623, 48658, 48686, 48723, 48751, 48753, 48754
LNWR 7F 0–8–0	49079, 49293, 49314, 49342, 49350, 49373, 49377, 49414, 49425, 49431, 49439, 49440, 49441
BR Class 2 2–6–0	78034
TOTAL: 86	
June 1966 (Final allocation)	
LMS Class 5 4–6–0	44771, 44831, 44866, 45001, 45065, 45310, 45405, 45448
LMS Class 2 2–6–0	46495, 46512, 46519, 46520
LMS 8F 2–8–0	48054, 48074, 48111, 48247, 48263, 48264, 48289, 48320, 48445, 48456, 48504, 48534, 48686, 48751, 48753
BR Class 4 4–6–0	75018, 75035, 75050
BR Class 2 2–6–0	78059
TOTAL: 31	
STAFFORD	BR Code 5C. Closed to steam 19 July 1965.
January 1957	
MR 2F 4–4–0	40443, 40461, 40583, 40646, 40678
LMS Class 4 2–6–4T	42309, 42345, 42346, 42347, 42418, 42421, 42425, 42538, 42562, 42578
LMS 'Jinty' 3F 0–6–0T	47359, 47588, 47590, 47606, 47649, 47653, 47665
LMS 8F 2–8–0	48263, 48727
LNWR 7F 0–8–0	48922, 49047, 49048, 49115, 49158, 49198, 49229, 49410
TOTAL: 32	
September 1961	
LMS Class 4 2–6–4T	42069, 42309, 42327, 42389
LMS 'Jinty' 3F 0–6–0T	47310, 47359, 47475, 47588, 47590, 47649, 47665
LMS 8F 2–8–0	48174, 48366, 48453, 48705, 48755, 48762
LNWR 7F 0–8–0	49357, 49377
TOTAL: 19	
July 1965 (Final allocation)	
LMS Class 5 4–6–0	44813, 44963, 45110, 45147, 45374
LMS 'Jinty' 3F 0–6–0T	47359, 47665
LMS 8F 2–8–0	48174, 48602
TOTAL: 9	

3

Modernisation

The Trent Valley Railway underwent significant changes as a result of proposals under the 1955 'Modernisation Plan', which involved electrification of the London Midland Region's West Coast Main Line between Euston and Liverpool/Manchester, and the GJR line from Stafford through Wolverhampton (High Level), Birmingham (New Street) and Coventry to Rugby. Although the scheme had received government approval, it was to be embroiled in financial and political controversy throughout the construction programme, which caused some delay and disruption while difficulties were resolved.

Under the 'Modernisation Plan' BR was to bring its railway system up to date by replacing its steam locomotives (many being less than five years old at this time) with new diesel and electric traction, and by making substantial investment in the infrastructure after years of neglect. Electrification of the East and West Coast Main Lines was envisaged, along with some areas in the Home Counties. The East Coast project was shelved until the 1980s, but London–Midland electrification went ahead at a scheduled cost of £118 million. These costs were to include substantial track improvements, resignalling, full electrification and completely new stations at Euston, Manchester (London Road) (renamed Manchester Piccadilly), Birmingham (New Street), Coventry and Stafford, as well as substantial refurbishment of others. As far as the TVR was concerned, Tamworth station was completely rebuilt at a cost of £200,000, opening on 24 September 1962. Efficient mail and parcels exchange facilities were major factors in the new station's design. Its future as a mail exchange point seemed assured, but this role was to cease in March 1967 when electrification was completed and mail trains were diverted over the L&B and GJR routes via Birmingham. Full electrification of the WCML was planned to be completed by 1964.

Electrification on BR was nothing new, as much of the Southern Region was already operated by the 750 volt DC third rail system, and the 1,500 volt DC overhead wire system was in operation on the ex-LNER Sheffield–Woodhead Tunnel–Manchester line. The latter system was favoured by the British Transport Commission but in the event the 25kv, 50Hz AC system was adopted for West Coast electrification, following a successful demonstration of its economy in installation costs and traction performance by the French. A test bed conversion of the Lancaster–Morecambe–Heysham line also showed superiority over the LNER system.

Work on the WCML electrification scheme began in 1957, the section between Manchester and Crewe being the first section to be so converted. By December of that year the West Midlands press eagerly announced LM Region plans to spend

£5½ million over the next five or six years, preparing track and infrastructure in the Stafford, Lichfield, Walsall and Wolverhampton areas for electrification, which included demolition and rebuilding of Stafford station, deep ballasting of track and the introduction of long welded rail in the region. Stafford station reconstruction work began in 1959. On 6 October BR announced that from the 25th of that month engineering work on the TVR would result in complete closure every weekend from midnight Saturday/Sunday to 5am Monday for the next two years. Trains running at these times were to be diverted via the GJR line through Bushbury (near Wolverhampton), Bescot, Stechford and Coventry, adding 35 minutes to journey times. Stations at Lichfield, Tamworth and Nuneaton were to be connected to Stafford by special bus services.

By September 1960 the Manchester–Crewe section of LM electrification was complete, giving the new electric locomotives just enough mileage to demonstrate a haulage, acceleration and sustained speed capacity which were better than anything else BR could offer. However, on government orders electrification of the WCML was brought to a halt as budgeted costs had rocketed from £118 million to beyond £160 million, owing to inflation and the unforeseen costs of rebuilding bridges with enlarged clearances for overhead wires. Minister of Transport Ernest Marples also put a stop to the reconstruction of Stafford station, which was left half demolished, and littered with builders' huts, until the following spring when the Conservative government gave grudging permission to resume WCML electrification.

With delays to electrification work, steam traction continued to head trains over the TVR right up to 14 June 1964, with 'Princess-Royal', 'Duchess' and BR 'Britannia' Pacifics very common sights over the route. Their numbers decreased as English Electric Type 4 1Co-Co1 (later Class 40) diesel-electric locomotives took over from steam haulage on important Euston–Glasgow and Euston–Holyhead expresses in the 1960s. The first modern diesel-electric locomotive to appear on the TVR was the prototype 3,300hp Co-Co English Electric 'Deltic' which was used for evaluation purposes from 1955 on Liverpool (Lime Street)–Euston expresses, usually the Up 'Shamrock' and Down 'Merseyside Express'. Successful evaluation led to construction of further examples, which went to the East Coast Main Line where they found considerable fame operating Kings Cross–Edinburgh expresses. Another experimental English-Electric locomotive, the Co-Co diesel-electric no. DP2, was introduced to the WCML in May 1962. Similar in appearance to the 'Deltic', it had a very short life on the route. Local services over the TVR began to be operated by new Diesel Multiple Unit sets from the late 1950s.

When approval for the continuation of electrification was given in the spring of 1961, work on Stafford station recommenced and electrification southward from Crewe was restarted. The new Stafford station, a modern concrete structure, was officially opened on 31 December 1962, only one week before inauguration of electric services between Stafford, Crewe, Manchester and Liverpool. Electrification on the TVR was then started, overhead catenaries appearing south of Stafford in 1962. The first section, between Stafford and Nuneaton, was completed and energised on 2 March 1964. The section between Nuneaton and Rugby was opened to electric trains from 30 November 1964. The remainder of the route to Euston was completed on 2 January 1966, and the Rugby–Birmingham–Stafford section was fully electrified a year later. The Colwich–Stone line, as part of the Potteries electrification, was energised on 6 March 1967 after being closed for three years. At Rugby an electric traction feeder station was located at the point where the TVR and Birmingham lines divide. Two CEGB-owned 18.75MVA 132:25kv transformers, operating in parallel, supplied traction power as far as Nuneaton.

From March 1964, when the Stafford–Nuneaton section became electric train operated, passenger services booked to pass Nuneaton had to stop for locomotive changing. Nuneaton shed crews were used on passenger workings between Nuneaton and Euston. As Nuneaton was a freight shed, crews had to learn the road to Euston on English Electric Type 4s. Local trains were Electric Multiple Units operated between Stafford and Nuneaton, passengers changing to DMUs for the remainder of their journeys to Rugby. Once electrification was complete as far as Rugby, locomotive changing took place there until the remainder of the line to London was finished. EMU trains operated local services all the way through from Stafford to Rugby.

When the Rugby–Birmingham line was being prepared for electrification, all Euston–Birmingham trains ran to Nuneaton (Trent Valley) and were then diesel-hauled to Birmingham along the MR route, with the electric locomotive still attached. A bus service was provided for passengers heading for Coventry, as this alternative route avoided the city.

By the late 1960s the TVR had a virtually new railway, essentially the one that is still in existence today. However, no further investment has been forthcoming and the issue at present is what to do about an infrastructure that needs substantial finance to bring the TVR, along with the rest of the West Coast Main Line, up to date.

An electrified Rugby station as seen from the power box on 6 May 1988. The station had already undergone some changes before electrification. In 1957 a new flyover was built, at a cost of £870,000, to the north of the station to eliminate surface crossing of the Up Birmingham line with TVR tracks. Birmingham trains were to have direct access to the main Up fast line and Up goods line, but the existing flat junction was retained until much later to allow Up Birmingham trains to gain the Up slow line without crossing the path of the trains on the Up TVR fast line. This flyover, in reinforced concrete, was brought into use on 17 September 1962. Rugby station also had the new power box, which became fully operational on 27 September 1964, and covered the TVR as far as Brinklow (along with the L&B to Coventry and the Northampton loop). As a result Brinklow signal-box was closed on 14 September. *(Revd D. Hardy)*

BR Bo-Bo diesel-electric locomotive no. 25109 is seen on a spoil train at Nuneaton station on 27 November 1981. Like the steam engines before them, many of these diesel locomotives have disappeared from the railway network and are now museum pieces. *(Revd D. Hardy)*

BR Class 87 Bo-Bo electric locomotive no. 87005 *City of London* passing through Nuneaton on 27 November 1981 a the head of the royal train. Also in view is 0–6–0 diesel shunter no. 08635, with Roy Marsden as driver, and anothe defunct diesel-electric locomotive, Class 31 Co-Co no. 31226. *(Revd D. Hardy)*

Passing a derailed Freightliner wagon at Nuneaton is one of the ill-fated Advanced Passenger Trains, nos 370002 and 370006 on 27 November 1981. Developed in the 1970s, the APT was designed for 150mph running over the tight curves and steep gradients of the WCML. A unique tilting mechanism was designed to allow the train to take the many curves at high speed, which would allow continuous high average speeds, thereby improving timings between London and Glasgow. Built at Derby, the streamlined APT had a 4,000hp power car at one end and a driving trailer at the other, with a ten-coach formation between. Three APT sets were constructed and dispatched to the WCML for trials in 1978, where 125mph running was expected, giving a London–Glasgow journey time of some 4½ hours, 45 minutes faster than the schedule then possible. Several design faults were found during the trials, although the special tilting mechanism seemed to work perfectly. However, when the train operated its first passenger services in 1981 the tilting of the APT over curves caused some discomfort for those travelling on the train, and all the APT sets were withdrawn, never to return to BR metals. One APT set has been preserved at Crewe Heritage Centre as a reminder of what might have been. The APT experiment was not a total failure and some of its features, notably the bogies, were incorporated into new Class 90 and 91 electric locomotives. The APT also showed that 'push-pull' operation could be undertaken, eliminating the need for engines to 'run round' at termini. Ironically, Virgin Trains, who took over the franchise for the WCML in 1997, have imported 'Pendelino' trains, which have tilting mechanisms and are designed to run at 150mph, although this may not be possible until the whole of the WCML has been expensively updated. Indeed, such is the state of the route that Virgin Trains are to receive some £100 million in compensation from Railtrack because of their inability to update the route. *(Revd D. Hardy)*

Electric Bo-Bo locomotive no. 87034 *William Shakespeare* passes a derailed Freightliner wagon at Nuneaton on 27 November 1981. Nuneaton lost its large signal-boxes when electrification arrived, and the old semaphore signals were replaced all along the TVR with four-aspect colour light signals as electrification progressed. All the goods yards on the TVR disappeared with the coming of the modern system, freight traffic being concentrated at Crewe, and many lines that formed junctions with the TVR also closed. *(Revd D. Hardy)*

Falling snow at Nuneaton station, with Class 47 Co-Co no. 47186 on an Up freight at 11.24am on 11 December 1981. *(Revd D. Hardy)*

Class 87 electric locomotive no. 87015 *Howard of Effingham* passing through Nuneaton station with a Down express at 1.32pm on 21 January 1983. Nuneaton station had its refreshment rooms shut down on 22 July 1965. Since 1960 these rooms had been run by the Nuneaton Railway Servants' Society, but they had lost customers when a tunnel under the station was closed. This tunnel had long been used as a short cut by the local population, who made use of the station facilities. Only a couple of years before two faces of the station clock had been removed and in 1971 the tracks in the substantial marshalling yards were ripped up. *(Revd D. Hardy)*

A night view at Nuneaton with Class 50 Co-Co diesel-electric locomotive no. 50004 at the head of an Up Freightliner train at 8.15pm on 21 January 1983. *(Revd D. Hardy)*

A general view of the electrified system at Nuneaton with Class 86 locomotive no. 86242 *James Kennedy G.C.* at the head of a Down express at 3.22pm on 7 October 1983. *(Revd D. Hardy)*

At the north end of Nuneaton station is another now-defunct diesel-electric locomotive, 'Peak' Type 4 1 Co-Co 1 no. 45009 at the head of a four-coach passenger train at 11.53am on 28 September 1984. *(Revd D. Hardy)*

An unusual sight at this time was the High Speed Train, with power cars 43121 and 43159, seen here on a summer-only service to Paignton, Devon, departing from Nuneaton at 9.37am. These sets were to become a more common sight on the TVR when they were introduced on the 'Irish Mail' in 1990 to avoid the need to change traction at Crewe, the sets having been made redundant on the East Coast Main Line following electrification. Introduction of HST sets reduced journey times between Holyhead and Euston by as much as 20 minutes. *(Revd D. Hardy)*

Class 58, BREL Type 5 Co-Co no. 58031 coming off the Coventry branch at 7.02pm on 4 July 1986. *(Revd D. Hardy)*

Diesel shunter no. 08928 at Abbey Junction signal-box on the last day of working, 6 April 1984. *(Revd D. Hardy)*

The same engine at Nuneaton on 6 April 1984, with driver Roy Marsden. *(Revd D. Hardy)*

Two-coach 'Sprinter' train no. 156403 at Nuneaton Abbey Junction at 7.25pm on 8 July 1988. These trains were relatively new at this time and were used on local trains to Coventry. *(Revd D. Hardy)*

A pair of Class 20 Bo-Bo diesel-electric locomotives, some of the earliest diesel-electric types to be introduced by BR and now virtually extinct. Nos 20187 and 20172 haul 0–6–0 diesel shunter no. 08103 towards the TVR from Birmingham at Abbey Junction (Code OX 77) on 22 April 1983. Behind the leading Class 20 is the branch to Market Harborough, then in use to bring railway ballast from Judkin's sidings. *(Revd D. Hardy)*

Class 47 locomotive no. 47019 with an Up Freightliner train (4L69) at Abbey Junction on 8 July 1988. *(Revd D. Hardy)*

Class 08 0–6–0 diesel shunter no. 08647 resting at Abbey Junction on 27 August 1982. *(Revd D. Hardy)*

An unidentified Class 86 electric locomotive in 'InterCity' raspberry ripple livery passes the well-preserved Jacobean-style main station building at Atherstone with an Up passenger train on 13 May 1988. Atherstone, along with Polesworth and Rugeley stations, became an unmanned halt in the autumn of 1972. Waiting facilities were reduced to 'bus shelter'-type structures and ticket sales ceased, passengers paying their fares on the trains. *(Revd D. Hardy)*

The main platform at Atherstone, at the Nuneaton end, on 25 September 1981. Four-aspect colour light signalling can be seen in the foreground. *(Revd D. Hardy)*

The modern signal-box at Atherstone in 1988, with signalman Paul Lewis at the door. *(Revd D. Hardy)*

The exterior of Atherstone station on 25 September 1981. All the windows are boarded up, no doubt because of vandalism. There are no station staff to keep an eye on the place, giving it an air of neglect. *(Revd D. Hardy)*

Two views of the signal-box at Polesworth in 1988. It looks somewhat out of place among the modern technology of the new electric railway. *(Revd D. Hardy)*

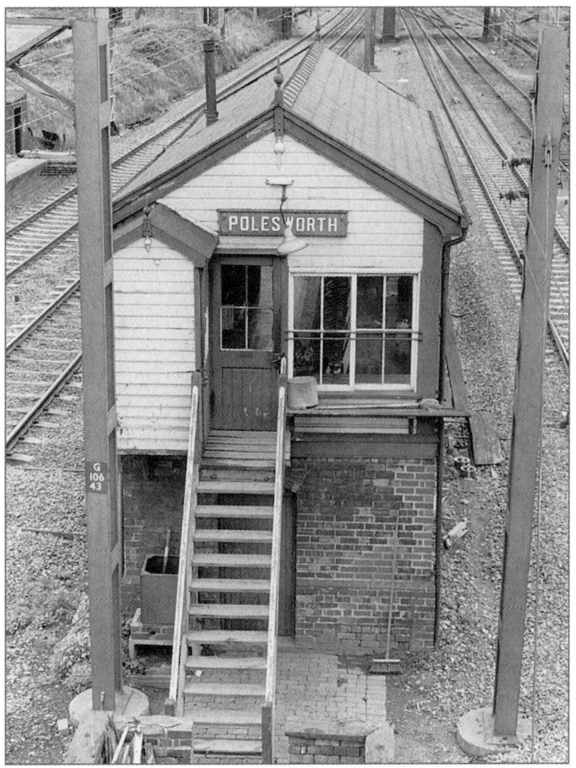

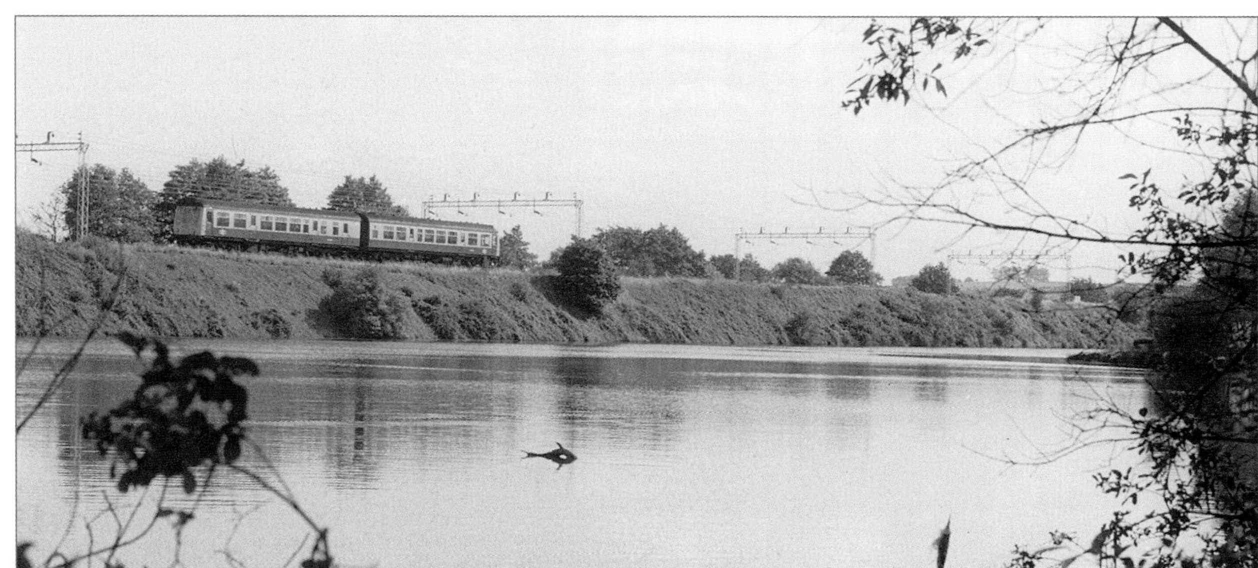

A very attractive view of the TVR just north of Polesworth with a diesel multiple unit train passing under the wires with a local service on 11 September 1987. As the last years of the twentieth century dawned it became obvious that substantial investment was needed to bring the WCML, and the TVR, up to date. The Conservative government was re-elected in 1992 and, after years of restricted railway expenditure, approved such investment in the November 1993 budget. The new administration, which had been busy privatising public industries since first elected in 1979, turned its privatisation spotlight on to British Rail. In April 1994 the whole railway system came under the control of Railtrack as part of the privatisation plans. However, owing to the poor state of the railway system along the WCML, plans to privatise this route were shelved. By 1997, though, things were different and Virgin Trains announced that they were to take the franchise to run WCML expresses, which included those running along the TVR. Ever since then, Virgin Trains have had to take a lot of blame for poor services along the WCML, much of which is not the company's fault but is the result of underinvestment by Railtrack, itself going into receivership in 2002, the Labour government taking control and making the running of the railway non-profit-making. *(Revd D. Hardy)*

Demolition of one of the trackside buildings at Tamworth Low Level station on 26 February 1988. *(Revd D. Hardy)*

The signal-box at Lichfield (Trent Valley), 29 July 1988. *(Revd D. Hardy)*

The rebuilt Stafford station looking north. In 1985 Stafford took on the role of a locomotive changing point, a function not enjoyed here since LNWR days, when Crewe station layout was remodelled, causing closure to all except local traffic. While work at Crewe was under way, all expresses bypassed the station using the freight line, rejoining the main line beyond Crewe. Any trains requiring a change of traction had to go to Stafford. In the same period major track remodelling was undertaken at Rugby to allow two-way working through the station and over the flyover to Birmingham. Work is still ongoing to bring the WCML and the TVR up to date and will not be completed until 2006–8 when, it is hoped, new Virgin trains will be able to operate at 150mph. Until then, a maximum speed of 125mph will be allowed. *(Author's Collection)*

NAMED TRAINS OPERATING OVER THE TVR IN THE 1950S

'The Royal Scot'	Euston–Glasgow/Edinburgh
'The Midday Scot'	Euston–Glasgow/Edinburgh
'The Caledonian'	Euston–Glasgow
'The Royal Highlander'	Euston–Inverness
'The Irish Mail'	Euston–Holyhead (for Dublin)
'The Emerald Isle Express'	Euston–Holyhead (for Dublin)
'The Welshman'	Euston–Llandudno/Pwllheli/Portmadoc (summer season only)
'The Comet'	Euston–Manchester, via Stoke-on-Trent
'The Mancunian'	Euston–Manchester
'The Lancastrian'	Euston–Manchester
'The Red Rose'	Euston–Liverpool
'The Merseyside Express'	Euston–Liverpool
'The Manxman'	Euston–Liverpool (for the Isle of Man)
'The Shamrock'	Euston–Liverpool (for Ireland)
'The Ulster Express'	Euston–Heysham (for Belfast)
'The Lakes Express'	Euston–Workington/Windermere

Named Trains over the TVR 1992–3 (electric-hauled)

'The Royal Scot'	Euston–Glasgow
'The Night Caledonian'	Glasgow–Euston
'The Manchester Pullman'	Euston–Manchester
'The Merseyside Pullman'	Euston–Liverpool
'The Lancashire Pullman'	Euston–Lancaster
'The Irish Mail'	Euston–Holyhead (HST diesel-electric)
'The Welsh Dragon/Y Ddraig Gymreig'	Euston–Holyhead (HST diesel-electric)

Chronology

6 May 1833	London & Birmingham Railway and Grand Junction Railway authorised.
4 July 1837	Grand Junction Railway opened.
24 June 1838	London & Birmingham Railway opened with a limited service (opened fully 17 September).
21 July 1845	Trent Valley Railway authorised.
14 April 1846	Trent Valley Railway purchased by the London & Birmingham Railway, the Grand Junction Railway, and the Manchester & Birmingham Railway.
16 July 1846	The London & North Western Railway formed.
15 September 1847	Trent Valley Railway partially opened (opened fully 1 December).
1 December 1847	Greenwich Mean Time adopted throughout the LNWR, coincidental with the transfer of Post Office mail trains from the L&B and GJR route, via Birmingham, to the Trent Valley route.
3 July 1871	Lichfield Trent Valley new station opened, replacing Lichfield South Staffordshire railway station.
14 August 1871	Bulkington–Rugby Up slow line opened.
27 January 1873	Nuneaton–Bulkington Up goods line opened.
1 June 1876	Nuneaton–Rugby Up slow line opened to passenger trains.
18 May 1877	Milford and Brocton station opened to passengers (opened to goods traffic on 22 January 1882).
1 October 1877	Armitage station opened to goods traffic.
8 November 1885	Rugby station–Trent Valley Junctions: four lines opened.
30 June 1890	Tamworth (Amington) Down loop opened.
26 July 1898	Stafford–Milford and Brocton section quadrupled.
1 July 1901	Atherstone–Tamworth partly quadrupled. Interior layout of Atherstone station modernised.
6 June 1909	Nuneaton–Hartshill Siding Down slow line opened.
13 February 1910	Attleborough Sidings–Nuneaton Down slow line opened.

30 December 1913 to 24 September 1915	Nuneaton station enlarged and partly rebuilt.
1 January 1923	LNWR and Trent Valley Railway became part of the LMS at 'Grouping'.
18 May 1931	Bulkington station closed.
1 January 1948	Nationalisation of the railways under the 1947 Transport Act; the Trent Valley Railway becomes part of the new London Midland Region of British Railways.
6 March 1950	Milford and Brocton station closed to passengers.
16 September 1957	Brinklow, Shilton and Colwich stations closed to passengers.
7 March 1960	Milford and Brocton closed to goods traffic.
13 June 1960	Armitage station closed.
24 September 1962	New station opened at Tamworth at a cost of £200,000.
2 March 1964	Electrification of Trent Valley Railway between Stafford and Nuneaton completed.
4 January 1965	Trent Valley Railway fully electrified.
6 March 1967	Mail trains lost to the Trent Valley line; they are diverted over their original L&B and GJR route, via Birmingham, following full electrification of Birmingham lines. Tamworth ceases to be a mail transfer point.
2 October 1972	Atherstone, Polesworth, and Rugeley reduced to unstaffed stations.
21 June 1990	'InterCity' unveil plans to update the WCML (including the TVR).
1 April 1994	Trent Valley Railway track, installations and stations brought under the control of Railtrack as part of the government plans for railway privatisation.
May 1995	Bids for private franchises to run trains over the British Railway network are accepted.
23 August 1995	The government announces that plans to privatise the WCML have been shelved.
1997	Sir Richard Branson's Virgin Trains take over express services on the WCML.
2002	Railtrack goes into receivership, the Labour government taking control and running the system on a non-profit-making basis.